Make:

MINECRAFT
FOR MAKERS

Make:
MINECRAFT
FOR MAKERS

Minecraft in the Real World with LEGO,
3D Printing, Arduino, and More!

JOHN BAICHTAL

MAKER MEDIA™
SAN FRANCISCO, CA

Published by Maker Media, Inc., 1700 Montgomery Street, Suite 240, San Francisco, CA 94111

Maker Media books may be purchased for educational, business, or sales promotional use. Online editions are also available for most titles (safaribooksonline.com). For more information, contact our corporate/institutional sales department: 800-998-9938 or corporate@oreilly.com.

Publisher: Roger Stewart
Copy Editor and Proofreader: Elizabeth Welch, Happenstance Type-O-Rama
Interior Designer and Compositor: Maureen Forys, Happenstance Type-O-Rama
Cover Designer: Maureen Forys, Happenstance Type-O-Rama
Indexer: Valerie Perry, Happenstance Type-O-Rama
Circuit diagrams designed in Fritzing (Fritzing.org)

August 2017: First Edition

Revision History for the First Edition

2017-08-26 First Release

See oreilly.com/catalog/errata.csp?isbn=9781680453157 for release details.

978-1-680-45315-7

SAFARI® BOOKS ONLINE

Safari Books Online is an on-demand digital library that delivers expert content in both book and video form from the world's leading authors in technology and business. Technology professionals, software developers, web designers, and business and creative professionals use Safari Books Online as their primary resource for research, problem solving, learning, and certification training. Safari Books Online offers a range of plans and pricing for enterprise, government, education, and individuals. Members have access to thousands of books, training videos, and prepublication manuscripts in one fully searchable database from publishers like O'Reilly Media, Prentice Hall Professional, Addison-Wesley Professional, Microsoft Press, Sams, Que, Peachpit Press, Focal Press, Cisco Press, John Wiley & Sons, Syngress, Morgan Kaufmann, IBM Redbooks, Packt, Adobe Press, FT Press, Apress, Manning, New Riders, McGraw-Hill, Jones & Bartlett, Course Technology, and hundreds more. For more information about Safari Books Online, please visit us online.

HOW TO CONTACT US

Please address comments and questions to the publisher:

Maker Media
1700 Montgomery St. Suite 240
San Francisco, CA 94111

You can send comments and questions to us by email at books@makermedia.com.

Maker Media unites, inspires, informs, and entertains a growing community of resourceful people who undertake amazing projects in their backyards, basements, and garages. Maker Media celebrates your right to tweak, hack, and bend any Technology to your will. The Maker Media audience continues to be a growing culture and community that believes in bettering ourselves, our environment, our educational system—our entire world. This is much more than an audience, it's a worldwide movement that Maker Media is leading. We call it the Maker Movement.

To learn more about Make: visit us at makezine.com. You can learn more about the company at the following websites:

Maker Media: makermedia.com

Maker Faire: makerfaire.com

Maker Shed: makershed.com

Thanks to the many makers
around the world who, like me,
were inspired by Minecraft to
build things in real life.

Contents

Part 3: Arduino Projects

About the Author

JOHN BAICHTAL has written or edited over a dozen books, including the award-winning *Cult of LEGO* (No Starch Press, 2011), LEGO hacker bible *Make: LEGO and Arduino Projects* (Maker Media, 2012) with Adam Wolf and Matthew Beckler, as well as *Robot Builder: The Beginner's Guide to Building Robots* (Que, 2013) and *Hacking Your LEGO Mindstorms EV3 Kit* (Que, 2015). John lives in Minneapolis with his wife and three children.

Introduction

One of the many charms of Minecraft involves translating the real world into the computer realm. How many examples of this have we seen? There is a Minecraft Taj Mahal, Tower of London, Washington DC Capitol, and a million others ranging from famous buildings to one's childhood home.

Thanks to a simplified building system, anyone from beginners to experts can re-create these structures. Oftentimes the block-like nature of the Minecraft interface makes for awkward translations, but frequently these projects impress viewers with their faithfulness.

Ironically, many of the adorably awkward Minecraft elements—especially the most commonplace ones—have no parallel in the real world. Finding a precise, one-meter block of granite in a forest is not something you can expect to happen very often outside of Minecraft, yet it occurs all the time in-game. There is, therefore, a delightful disconnect between the two realms that fascinates many players.

The purpose of the book is to reverse the paradigm of re-creating real-world elements in-game. Instead we'll take those eccentric Minecraft elements and introduce them to our world.

WHAT YOU'LL LEARN

This book consists of nine projects that will guide you along this approach:

CHAPTER 1: ITEM FRAME WITH DIAMOND SWORD

This wall-mounted decoration evokes a fanciful Minecraft element, an "Item Frame" that stores one object and displays it much like a painting. The chapter begins with a treatise on how to measure in-game objects and translate them to the real world.

CHAPTER 2: LEGO MINECRAFT BLOCK

The world's favorite toy, LEGO evokes a similar feel to Minecraft because you also use blocks/bricks to re-create the real world. LEGO even offers numerous Minecraft-inspired sets, further reinforcing that point. In this chapter I'll show you how to build the classic Minecraft block using LEGO bricks.

CHAPTER 3: MINECRAFT CHESS SET

In addition to geological elements, Minecraft includes a number of monsters like zombies and wolves, collectively known as mobs. In this chapter I'll show you how to re-create these mobs in the real world, in order to make them pieces of a chess set.

CHAPTER 4: LED-LIT MINECRAFT BLOCK

The iconic Minecraft element, the ore block has become synonymous with the game for many people. In this chapter you'll build such a cube, equipped with an LED and a battery pack so that you can make it light up.

CHAPTER 5: REDSTONE LAMP

The next project builds off of the glowing block idea, literally! In the game there exists formations of naturally occurring glowstone blocks. The Glowstone Chandelier resembles such a formation, conveniently sized for your home.

CHAPTER 6: LIGHT-UP CHESS BOARD

Those who created a chess set in Chapter 3 likely are gnashing their teeth over the lack of a proper board upon which to play. This project consists of redstone lamp blocks serving as white and obsidian blocks representing black.

CHAPTER 7: FLICKERING LED JACK O'LANTERN

You'll level up once again by employing the Arduino microcontroller to build a Minecraft jack o'lantern with a realistic flickering flame effect.

CHAPTER 8: NIGHT AND DAY CLOCK

For the next project, you'll re-create an in-game clock that rotates a disk decorated to look like night and day. Your Arduino will connect to a real-time clock (RTC) module to get an accurate sense of the time, with a stepper motor turning the disk.

CHAPTER 9: ROBOT CREEPER

The final project consists of a robotic chassis decorated to look like Minecraft's signature mob, the Creeper. Its head turns with the help of a stepper motor, and it rolls around on motorized wheels.

I conclude with an appendix that guides Arduino newbies through that great platform's interface.

Good luck and thanks for reading!

PART 1

Basic Projects

Item Frame with Diamond Sword

1

In Minecraft, one technique you can employ to store equipment is an Item Frame, which looks like a painting of whatever is stored in it. Figure 1-1 shows the game element with a diamond sword contained within it—just the thing you need to protect your house from the next zombie incursion. In this chapter you'll re-create this frame using wood and paint, creating a decoration for your real-life house to match one you might have in your Minecraft house.

FIGURE 1-1: An Item Frame found in Minecraft

To learn how to craft an Item Frame in Minecraft, search for it in the Official Minecraft Wiki at minecraft.gamepedia.com.

TRANSLATING MINECRAFT TO THE REAL WORLD

Before you translate anything from Minecraft, it helps to analyze the digital version of the object to get a sense of dimensions and proportions. You do this by looking at an item's scale and color. Since Minecraft simulates the real world, you can easily translate between the two realms—as long as you know the rules.

Scale

Your character in Minecraft, known as Steve, is considered to be of average human height, though considerably blockier and wider than a typical person. Steve is shorter than two blocks but taller than one, which gives you the assumed block dimension of one meter per side. Using this one-meter measure, you can pretty much compute the dimensions of anything found in the game. Figure 1-2 shows Steve next to two blocks.

FIGURE 1-2: Steve measures up next to two blocks.

The 16×16 Grid

Blocks are further divided into a 16×16 grid of smaller squares. Many objects aren't block-shaped, but they usually employ a similar grid to keep the game's look consistent. Some blocks have a different pattern depending on which side you're looking at, but they all follow the 16×16 pixel format.

Figure 1-3 shows a coal ore block, with black and shades of gray giving the block the signature Minecraft look. Matching this grid enables you to more accurately re-create game elements like the frame.

FIGURE 1-3: A coal ore block serves as a typical Minecraft block.

Figure 1-4 shows an illustration of one face of a coal ore block. If you were re-creating such a block in the real world, you'd want to make a diagram—perhaps on graph paper—to help you paint the thing. Later in this chapter I'll offer suggestions on how to decorate the Item Frame using a similar technique.

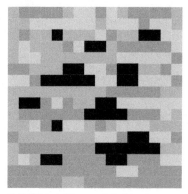

FIGURE 1-4: Diagram of a block

Color

Minecraft uses the 16×16 grid and variously colored squares to give game elements a degree of surface variation.

True to the game's low-resolution approach, Minecraft uses a limited color palette, with most elements having only a few colors—eight or fewer, in most cases, including shades of a single color. In Figure 1-5 you can see a diamond ore block, which looks exactly like the coal ore block except with blue instead of black.

As you can see, not many shades of color are used—only three, in fact, plus white and four shades of gray. When you buy paint, you don't need to get a separate container for each shade seen. Very often, you can mix shades together to make the new colors. For instance, the diamond ore's light blue can be made by mixing the darker blue and white together.

FIGURE 1-5: Typical Minecraft colors

Examining the Item Frame and Sword

With all that in mind, we must create a real-world design for the Item Frame and sword combo. Looking at the game element (Figure 1-6), you can see that the frame is stuck onto a one-meter block, and it's apparent there are two squares on each side of the frame where you can see the background block. Therefore, with each square equaling $1/16$ meters, or 2.46″, the frame itself would be 29.5″ on a side.

However, this seems kind of big to me. I'd like to make my frame only 12″ on a side, with each square equaling one inch. That means the frame itself has a width of one square, and the interior of the frame measures 10×10.

As you can see in Figure 1-6, the sword keeps the same jags and angles it did as a full-sized game element, and they are simply shrunk down. To create that element, we'll simply make a full-sized design and shrink it down as needed.

FIGURE 1-6: Examining an in-game Item Frame

BUILDING THE ITEM FRAME

With the design in mind, it's time to build the frame. It consists of a 12×12 panel of plywood, bordered in 1″ strips of wood, and then decorated with paint and a wooden Minecraft sword. You can see the finished project in Figure 1-7. It's the perfect decoration for any lair!

FIGURE 1-7: **Re-creating the frame in the real world**

Tools and Materials

I used the following to build my Item Frame:

- 12″×12″ piece of ¼″ plywood
- 9″×9″ piece of ⅛″ plywood
- Two 12″ and two 10″ pine boards, 1″ wide by 0.75″ thick
- Picture-hanging hardware
- Sandpaper; a variety of grits for smoothing down cut wood
- Wood glue; I used Titebond carpenter's glue
- Masking tape
- Spray paint: Rust-Oleum, satin, in Espresso and Nutmeg colors (it's available at the Home Depot)
- Craft paint; I used Craft Smart acrylic paint, with Rich Brown and Ground Cinnamon for the brown colors and Mediterranean and Pacific Coast for the blues
- Saw; either a hand saw or a power saw

Make the Item Frame

Let's begin with the frame itself, after which we'll tackle the sword.

1. Cut the Backing

I happened to have a one-foot piece of plywood handy, a leftover board from another project. However, if you're not so lucky you'll have to cut it yourself. This is the sort of thing you'll have to cut using a hand saw or a power saw. If you don't have access to such a tool, you can always get the folks at the hardware store to cut a piece of wood you just bought. Figure 1-8 shows my board, ready for decoration.

FIGURE 1-8: **Begin with a piece of plywood.**

2. Paint the Backing

Before you attach the frame, you'll want to paint the backing. You can either paint it a nondescript brown or follow the pattern of the game object. I began by using spray paint to cover the wood (Figure 1-9), and then went in with craft paint to add some surface detail. Paint the background color first, allow it to dry, tape off 1″ increments, and paint with darker shades of brown.

FIGURE 1-9: **Painting the wooden backing**

3. Cut the Wood Strips

Cut the 1″ wooden strips into 12″ and 10″ lengths. There's no point in mitering the corners since it's all divided into 1″ squares anyway. Figure 1-10 shows a diagram of how the frame comes together.

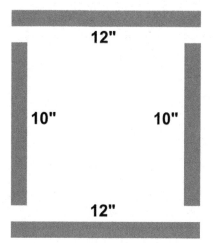
FIGURE 1-10: **Cut the pieces of frame.**

4. Paint the Frame

I gave the frame a basic coat of the "nutmeg" spray paint. As with the backing, I suggest painting the frame an overall color and then painting individual squares to make it more authentic. Figure 1-11 gives you a guide for colorizing your frame.

5. Glue the Frame

Glue and clamp the border to the backing, as seen in Figure 1-12. For added security you can screw in through the back, first making judicious pilot holes—you don't want to go all the way through!

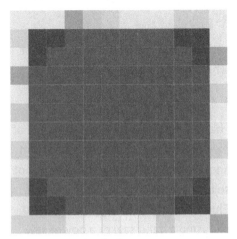

FIGURE 1-11: **Paint the frame.**

However, I didn't screw mine and it's holding together fine.

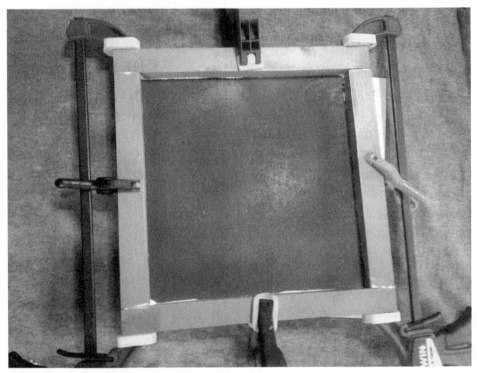

FIGURE 1-12: **Glue and clamp the frame.**

6. Add the Picture Hanger

Assuming you want to display your creation, add picture-hanging hardware (Figure 1-13) to the back using the screws that came with it. Note that the weird lines seen in the figure are left over from another project.

7. Trace the Sword Shape

Next, let's make the sword. Figure 1-14 shows the sword design as a series of squares. I have included this design in the online files for this book, downloadable at https://github.com/n1/MinecraftMakers. Simply print this design shrunk down to 9″ in length, which will make it the right size to fit into the 12″ frame.

8. Cut Out the Sword

If you have access to a laser cutter, the line drawing can be used to cut out a sword shape out of wood or plastic, as seen in Figure 1-15. At 100 percent it will output the full-sized (1-meter) Minecraft sword. For the 9″ sword used in the project, simply output the sword shape at 22.5 percent of the original size.

If you don't have access to such fancy equipment, the easiest way to make the sword is to print out the design on paper, shrunk down to the right size in the Print Setup window. Then spray-glue the printed design to a piece of plywood and cut out the design with a saw. You can sand off the glued-on paper when you're done.

FIGURE 1-13: Add picture-hanging hardware to the back.

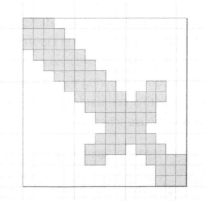

FIGURE 1-14: The Minecraft sword in all its pixelated glory

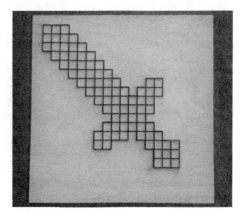

FIGURE 1-15: The laser-cut sword, ready for painting

9. Paint the Sword

Paint the sword a basic color; then tape off individual squares and paint them different shades, or simply do it freehand. Figure 1-16 shows the sword's color scheme.

You may find yourself struggling with choosing the right color to match the game element. Unfortunately, there is no definitive color-matching guide for Minecraft. One resource I discovered is design software giant Adobe's Color service (color.adobe.com), which helps with choosing color palettes. Searching for "Minecraft" on the site gives you any number of five-color palettes designed by the site's users, as seen in Figure 1-17. Each color comes with its hexadecimal and RGB codes, allowing you to interface with such other standards as Pantone, as well as in-house schemes.

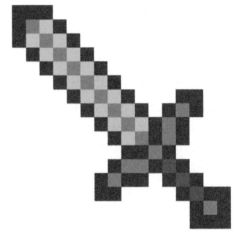

FIGURE 1-16: **Painting the sword**

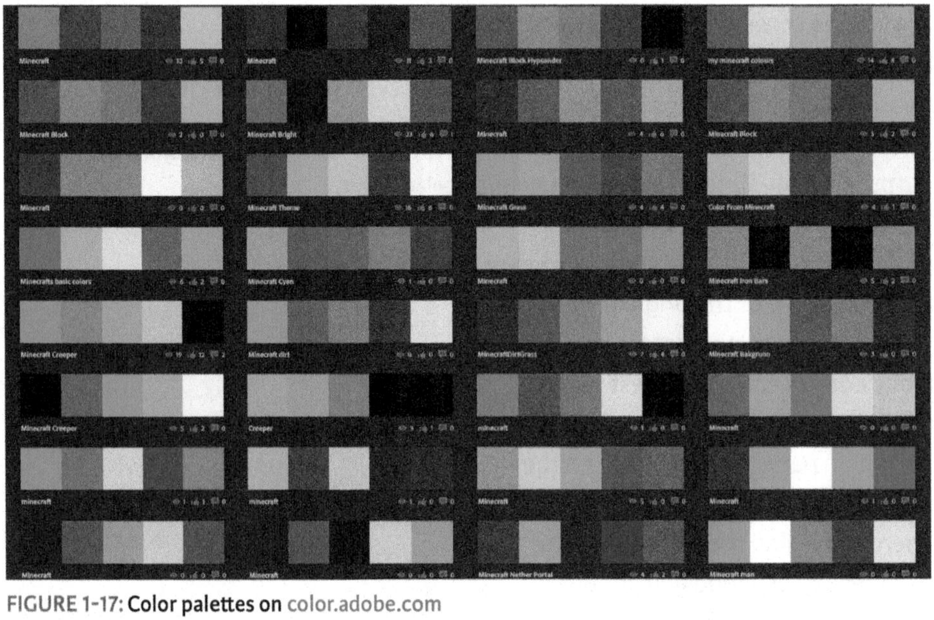

FIGURE 1-17: **Color palettes on** color.adobe.com

10. Attach the Sword to the Backing

Once dried, the sword is ready to glue to the backing, as seen in Figure 1-18. I simply applied wood glue to the unpainted side of the sword and then put heavy things on it until the glue dried. And with that we're done!

FIGURE 1-18: Gluing the sword to the backing

SUMMARY

While basic, this project introduced you to a number of important topics, not the least of which was the way Minecraft objects can be translated into the real world by measuring the squares and blocks of the game world. In Chapter 2, I'll show you how to translate Minecraft to the world's best building toy, LEGO.

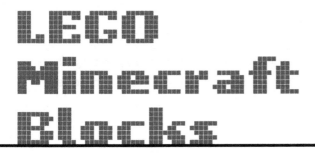
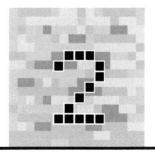

LEGO Minecraft Blocks

Minecraft fans frequently turn to LEGO to re-create their favorite game elements. Although not perfect for the job, the building set's bricks may be used to represent Minecraft's iconic blocks, like the ones seen in Figure 2-1. The companies have even teamed up to release a line of Minecraft-themed LEGO sets replicating some of the video game's locations and mobs.

You don't need a commercial Minecraft set to work with LEGO, however. This chapter describes how to build ore blocks out of LEGO using three techniques: tile elements on a six-plate cube, a large Emerald Ore block built out of LEGO bricks, and a small, brick-made Coal Ore block.

FIGURE 2-1: LEGO versions of Minecraft blocks

TRANSLATING MINECRAFT TO LEGO

Making a rectilinear shape in LEGO is a cinch: it turns out making a perfect(ish) cube, however, is rather challenging. Let's examine the classic LEGO brick to see what's going on.

Dimensions

To get a better idea of the challenge presented, look at the dimensions of the classic LEGO brick, seen in Figure 2-2. The brick's height is 9.6mm plus an additional 1.8mm for the stud. When I use the term "brick," it refers to a standard-height brick, whereas a "plate" is one-third the height of a normal brick. A flat "tile" has a smooth top and can fit on top of a standard LEGO element, but it is thinner than a plate.

A single-stud 1×1 brick is 8mm wide, minus 0.1mm wiggle room on each side, for a total of 7.8mm. So when you look at a 2×4 brick like the one in Figure 2-2, you get a width of 16mm and a length of 32mm, minus 0.2mm in both cases. This is necessary because building sets lacking such a tolerance make it more difficult to connect and disconnect elements.

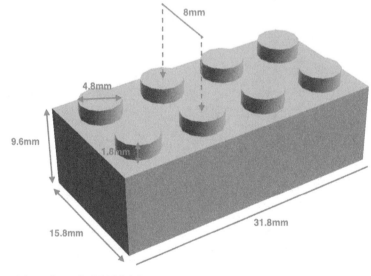

FIGURE 2-2: **Dimensions of a LEGO brick**

Studs themselves are 4.8mm wide and the distance between studs' centers is 8mm, matching the nominal width of a 1×1 element.

For the definitive word on LEGO measurements, check out Robert Cailliau's write-up at robertcailliau.eu/Lego/Dimensions/zMeasurements-en.xhtml.

How do you pile up LEGO bricks and plates so as to make a perfect square? Looking at Figure 2-3, you can see the solution. Using an 8×8 plate as a guide, you simply stack up six bricks and add a plate on the bottom and a flat tile on top, and you get exactly the dimension you're looking for.

LEGO elements are brilliantly, cleverly engineered but most of the time can't make perfect cubes. By stacking the bricks as you see here, however, you can do it. And it scales up, of course: a 4×4 cube uses three bricks plus a tile and a plate, whereas a 16×16 cube uses twelve.

FIGURE 2-3: **How do you make a cube with LEGO bricks?**

Simulating Colors

Minecraft is known for its limited color palette, with approximately 36 colors representing the world. This meshes well with LEGO, which also has a limited palette of around 50 colors (Figure 2-4), many of which have been discontinued temporarily or permanently. We are further hampered by the fact that not every element has been manufactured in every color. Fortunately, the game's palette consists primarily of commonplace colors, and these are well represented in the LEGO's offerings.

> **For more detailed information on colors in Minecraft, check out** minecraft.gamepedia.com/Map_item_format#Map_colors.

See this book's appendix, which breaks down the color scheme by RGB, Pantone, and more.

FIGURE 2-4: LEGO offers a rainbow of parts.

Where to Get LEGO Pieces

"How do I get more LEGO pieces?" This question has been encountered so often by LEGO fans that it's almost a cliché. The following are some likely sites for purchasing more bricks:

- bricklink.com: The ultimate site for buying and selling new and used LEGO sets, figures, and parts. I suppose you could say it's the eBay of bricks.
- brickowl.com: A similar marketplace offering unusual and commonplace elements.
- ebay.com: The literal eBay, but you won't find individually available parts the way you can on Bricklink or Brick Owl. Rather, you'll find giant buckets of elements sold off (one imagines) by short-sighted parents after their kids lose interest.
- shop.lego.com: Or go to the motherlode. Lego's Pick-a-Brick online and physical stores offer an array of parts. You'll find a better variety of parts on Bricklink or Brick Owl, but this is still a great resource.

BUILDING LEGO BLOCKS

I'm going to share two different methods for making the block. The two basic types are 1) using bricks to form the sides, and 2) using plates for the same purpose. Each technique has different advantages and disadvantages, and I'll show you how to make small (8×8) and big (16×16) versions of both.

8×8 Brick Coal Ore Block

The first re-creation downgrades the 16×16 resolution to 8×8, allowing for a simplified look that nevertheless evokes the Minecraft feel. The top and bottom are 8×8 plates, and the top is decorated with tiles to get the classic ore pattern.

If you recall from the section on making squares in LEGO, a perfect square would be the model pictured in Figure 2-5, minus one of the plates.

FIGURE 2-5: **The Coal Ore block, depicted in LEGO**

However, I wanted to keep the model as simple as possible. If you want to ditch that top 8×8 plate, I suggest filling up the interior of the cube with random bricks so that the flat tiles can sit flush with the walls' studs.

With the individual LEGO elements 9.6mm high but only 7.8mm wide, I was forced to fudge the ore pattern even further, dropping it down to 6 pixels high. I think this method does a great job of illustrating a Minecraft block, and it doesn't use as many elements as the other techniques I'll share in this chapter.

Parts

Gather the following elements to build your Coal Ore block:

- 2 dark stone gray 8×8 plates, P/N 4210802
- 8 black 1×1 bricks, P/N 300526
- 24 dark stone gray 1×1 bricks, P/N 4211098
- 12 light stone gray 1×1 bricks, P/N 300502
- 12 medium stone gray 1×1 bricks, P/N 4211389
- 16 black 1×2 bricks, P/N 300426
- 8 medium stone gray 1×2 bricks, P/N 3211388
- 20 light stone gray 1×2 bricks, P/N 300402
- 8 medium stone gray 1×3 bricks, P/N 4211428
- 4 light stone gray 1×3 bricks, P/N 362202
- 5 black 1×1 flat tiles, P/N 307026
- 9 dark stone gray 1×1 flat tiles, P/N 4210848
- 4 light stone gray 1×1 flat tiles, P/N 307021
- 5 medium stone gray 1×1 flat tiles, P/N 4211415
- 2 black 1×2 flat tiles, P/N 306926
- 5 light stone gray 1×2 flat tiles, P/N 306902
- 5 medium stone gray 1×2 flat tiles, P/N 4211414
- 1 dark stone gray 1×2 flat tile, P/N 4109959
- 2 black 1×3 flat tiles, P/N 4558170
- 3 medium stone gray 1×3 flat tiles, P/N 4558169

- Bricks (color irrelevant) to fill in the interior of the cube to eliminate the need for a top plate (optional)

Steps

Once you have assembled your heap of bricks, begin the assembly by following along with these steps.

1. Build the Sides

Figure 2-6 shows how to build one side of the Coal Ore block using the bricks specified in the previous list. Do this four times and combine them together to form a square.

FIGURE 2-6: **Build one of the sides out of bricks.**

2. Add Bottom and Top Plates

Attach 16×16 plates to the top and bottom of the brick assembly, as shown in Figure 2-7. If you want to keep it a perfect cube and skip the top plate, now is the time to fill in the interior with bricks. It doesn't matter what color; the important thing is to make a flat surface of studs aligned with the topmost row of bricks.

FIGURE 2-7: **Add top and bottom plates.**

3. Add Tiles to Top

Once you've either added the plate or filled in the cube with other bricks, it's time to add the tiles. Figure 2-8 shows how to place them to re-create my design.

FIGURE 2-8: **Decorate the top with tiles.**

8×8 Plate Coal Ore Block

As you are undoubtedly thinking right now, why not just make a cube using six copies of the top of the previous version? And use bricks with studs on the side to attach the six plates together? One problem immediately presents itself: the edges are beveled (Figure 2-9) and don't form a Minecraft-friendly cube. In any case, here's how to make it.

Parts

Collect the following LEGO elements to build your 8×8 Plate Coal Ore block:

FIGURE 2-9: **A Coal Ore block made from plates**

- 6 dark stone gray 8×8 plates
- Eight 1×4 bricks with knobs, PN 30414
- 30 black 1×1 flat tiles, P/N 307026
- 54 dark stone gray 1×1 flat tiles, P/N 4210848
- 24 light stone gray 1×1 flat tiles, P/N 307021
- 30 medium stone gray 1×1 flat tiles, P/N 4211415
- 12 black 1×2 flat tiles, P/N 306926
- 30 light stone gray 1×2 flat tiles, P/N 306902
- 30 medium stone gray 1×2 flat tiles, P/N 4211414
- 6 dark stone gray 1×2 flat tiles, P/N 4109959
- 12 black 1×3 flat tiles, P/N 4558170
- 18 medium stone gray 1×3 flat tiles, P/N 4558169

Steps

Not unexpectedly, the assembly steps pretty much involve making sides and attaching them together.

1. Make One Side

Place tiles on the 8×8 plate to match the design shown in Figure 2-10.

2. Add Bricks with Studs

Place 1×4 bricks with studs on the backside of the 8×8 plate, as shown in Figure 2-11. You will use these to attach other sides of the cube at right angles. Eventually you'll use eight total.

FIGURE 2-10: **One side of the coal block**

3. Add More Sides

Build two more sides and attach them to the 1×4 bricks with studs, forming half of the cube. Figure 2-12 shows how it should look.

4. Finish Up

Keep adding 1×4 bricks with studs and sides. Figure 2-13 shows the model almost complete, missing only one side.

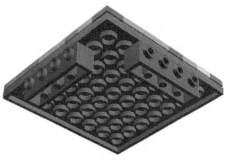

FIGURE 2-11: **Attach bricks with studs to the backside of the 8×8 plate.**

FIGURE 2-12: **Adding a second and a third side**

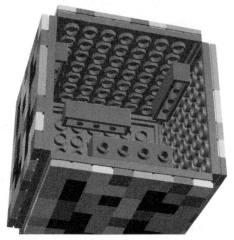

FIGURE 2-13: **Finishing the model**

16×16 Brick Emerald Ore Block

With the 8×8 versions of the blocks conquered, let's level up and tackle blocks twice as big, 16×16 studs. The first of these re-creates an Emerald Ore block, as shown in Figure 2-14. As you may have noticed, the 12 layers of bricks on the sides do not faithfully replicate the game element. Just as I did with the Coal Ore block, described earlier, I had to cut out some detail to fit 16 pixels of information into 12.

Similar to the Coal Ore version, I included an extra 16×16 plate at the top of the model, and this knocks it out of being an even cube. If that's a nonstarter, eliminate the top layer of bricks and replace it with a layer of plates.

FIGURE 2-14: **The Emerald Ore block measures 16×16 studs.**

Parts

You'll need the following LEGO elements:

- 2 dark stone gray 16×16 plates, P/N 91415
- 32 white 1×1 bricks, P/N 300501
- 60 dark green 1×1 bricks P/N 300528
- 32 earth green 1×1 bricks, P/N 4521915
- 48 medium stone gray 1×1 bricks, P/N 4211389
- 56 dark stone gray 1×1 bricks, P/N 4211098
- 16 light stone gray 1×2 bricks, P/N 300402
- 12 medium stone gray 1×3 bricks, P/N 4211428
- 24 medium stone gray 1×4 bricks, P/N 4211394
- 4 dark stone gray 1×4 bricks, P/N 4211103
- 9 white 1×1 flat tiles, P/N 307001
- 18 dark green 1×1 flat tiles, P/N 4558593
- 9 earth green 1×1 flat tiles, P/N 6055171

- 25 medium stone gray 1×1 flat tiles, P/N 4211415
- 14 dark stone gray 1×1 flat tiles, P/N 4210848
- 15 light stone gray 1×1 flat tiles, P/N 4210848
- 18 medium stone gray 1×2 flat tiles, P/N 4210848
- 21 dark stone gray 1×2 flat tiles, P/N 4109959
- 9 light stone gray 1×2 flat tiles, P/N 306902
- 7 medium stone gray 1×3 flat tiles, P/N 4210848
- 5 dark stone gray 1×3 flat tiles, P/N 4558169
- 4 medium stone gray 1×4 flat tiles, P/N 4211356
- 4 dark stone gray 1×4 flat files, P/N 4211053

As with the Coal Ore block, you may also want to fill in the interior with bricks and skip the top plate for a perfect cube.

Steps

As you might expect, the build process very much resembles building the brick version of the Coal Ore block. Let's get started!

1. Build the Sides

Figure 2-15a shows one of the sides, with each brick outlined so you can see its color and size. Figure 2-15b shows the reverse angle.

FIGURE 2-15a: One side of the Emerald Ore block

FIGURE 2-15b: A reverse angle

2. Add the Top and Bottom

Add top and bottom plates, as shown in Figure 2-16. Skip the top plate and fill in the interior to get a perfect cube.

3. Decorate the Top

As with the six-plate version, the top plate of the Emerald Ore block is covered in tiles. Figure 2-17 shows you how to finish your block.

FIGURE 2-16: **Add the top and bottom plates.**

FIGURE 2-17: **One side of the Emerald Ore block**

16×16 Plate Redstone Ore Block

The model seen in Figure 2-18 consists of six 16×16 plates (one stud per pixel!) covered with a veritable mountain of tiles: there are 1,536 studs to cover on the top, bottom, and sides. Okay, so that's a little excessive, but it's the most accurate way to build a Minecraft block in LEGO.

Parts

You'll need the following parts to build the project, with part quantities *per side*. Multiply by 6 if you want all six sides covered.

FIGURE 2-18: **Making a Redstone Ore block with LEGO plates**

- 1 dark stone gray 16×16 plate, P/N 91415
- 11 bright red 1×1 flat tiles, P/N 307021
- 11 dark red 1×1 flat tiles, P/N 4187196
- 26 medium stone gray 1×1 flat tiles, P/N 4211415
- 20 dark stone gray 1×1 flat tiles, P/N 4210848
- 5 bright red 1×2 flat tiles, P/N 306921
- 3 dark red 1×2 flat tiles, P/N 4165783
- 11 medium stone gray 1×2 flat tiles, P/N 4210848
- 2 dark stone gray 1×2 flat tiles, P/N 4109959
- 14 light stone gray 1×2 flat tiles, P/N 306902
- 15 medium stone gray 1×3 flat tiles, P/N 4211356
- 3 dark stone gray 1×3 flat tiles, P/N 4558169
- 7 medium stone gray 1×4 flat tiles, P/N 4211356
- 3 dark stone gray 1×4 flat files, P/N 4211053
- 3 dark stone gray 2×4 flat tiles, P/N 4560184
- Eight 1×4 bricks with knobs (PN 30414 is one example, but they will be hidden and any color will do). You'll need a maximum of 16 to build the whole cube.

Steps

To create the Redstone Ore block, follow these steps:

1. Decorate One Side of the Block

As with the smaller version, decorate one of the plates with the tiles, as shown in Figure 2-19.

FIGURE 2-19: **Adding tiles to one side of the block**

2. Add Bricks with Knobs

Take a 16×16 plate and add eight 1×4 bricks with knobs, as shown in Figure 2-20.

3. Add the Second Panel

Build a second panel and attach it to the other panel with the help of the 1×4 bricks with knobs, as shown in Figure 2-21.

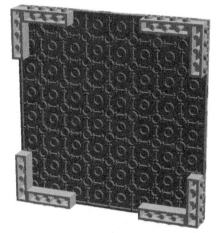
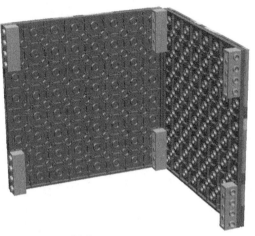

FIGURE 2-20: **Adding bricks with knobs**

FIGURE 2-21: **Add the second side.**

4. Finish the Build

Oh, heck, at this point you have it figured it out. Keep adding sides; Figure 2-22 shows the build with five sides in place.

FIGURE 2-22: **Add the rest of the sides.**

SUMMARY

In this chapter, you tackled two different methods for making Minecraft blocks in LEGO. In Chapter 3 you'll return to woodworking, making a Minecraft-inspired chess set out of thin pieces of wood, as well as using a 3D printer to make pieces out of plastic.

Minecraft Chess Set

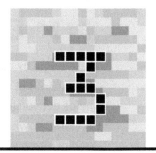

In this chapter I'm going to show you how to build a chess set, both in-game and real-world. Minecraft, as an essentially collaborative game, works perfectly as a platform for chess. You can build a board and challenge a friend to a game. When one player makes a move, he or she leaves a signal for the other person. Even if weeks go by before the opponent makes his or her move, the board will wait undisturbed.

I'll also show you how to bring the game into the real world by building a chess set out of wood or by 3D-printing one. You can see the set I built in Figure 3-1, a series of wooden pieces designed on the computer, cut out of eighth-inch plywood and painted with black or white paint.

FIGURE 3-1: You'll build a Minecraft-themed chess set.

BUILDING AN IN-GAME MINECRAFT CHESS SET

Let's begin by building a chess set within the game itself, like the one shown in Figure 3-2. Let's do this for the best possible reason: to play a game online! It also helps get you in the mood for chess before you build your set.

First, however, you'll need a board. A chess board can be quite simple: an 8×8 grid of alternating black and white blocks. When looking at the board, you should see a black square on the far left of the first row, and the queen should be positioned on her own color.

Now, follow along to see how I built my chess pieces.

FIGURE 3-2: First, we'll build an in-game chess set.

The Pieces

Although the real-life chess set makes use of Minecraft mobs (monsters) to differentiate pawns from rooks, the in-game version can't use mobs because they'd just wander off. As a consequence, the most obvious elements you could use are off limits.

The Kings

You pretty much have to make the king the biggest piece in the set (along with the queen) because he's important and wants everyone to know! I built the kings (Figure 3-3) with a pair of blocks, coal for black and quartz for white. Topping each piece is a head, a Wither Skull for black, and a Steve Head for white. In Creative mode, you can find these under the Decorations tab. If you are playing in Survival, you may need to substitute other elements because Wither Skulls and Steve Heads are quite rare.

FIGURE 3-3: The kings stand tall on a pair of blocks apiece.

I avoided using full-sized blocks for the chess pieces because I didn't want to clutter up the board. Ideally you should be able to see the square the piece is standing on. Due to limitations of available elements, I went with full-sized blocks for only kings and queens. Play around with the elements found under the Building tab, but don't be hesitant to check out the other menus.

The Queens

The queens (Figure 3-4) also sport blocks, but only one. Here I also introduce the core element of the pieces, the

FIGURE 3-4: The queens stand a head over two blocks high.

Anvil for black and Brewing Stand for white. With these I can have pieces smaller than a full block, a necessity for such a small board. As mentioned, it would just get too cluttered. For heads I used Zombie for black and Skeleton for white.

The Rooks

The rooks (Figure 3-5) are so simple it's ridiculous. I simply used banners of the color you might expect. The solution works in part because the vertical rectangle resembles the classic tower of a chess rook. You can find the banners menu in Minecraft by hitting R2 while in the Crafting menu.

FIGURE 3-5: Rooks—just use banners.

The Bishops

I got to have more fun creating the bishops. I set down their bases, a Brewing Stand for white and Anvil for black. Topping them are a Web and Hopper, respectively. Figure 3-6 shows what I built.

FIGURE 3-6: The bishops use the Web and Hopper to set them apart.

The Knights

By now the knights ought to be predictable: the go-to base, with the go-to head on top. Figure 3-7 shows them: Anvil with Zombie Head for black, Brewing Stand with Skeleton Head for white.

The Pawns

For the pawns I went simple: Flower Pots with Daisies for white and Cacti for black. I wanted them as small as possible so as to not clog up the board. Figure 3-8 shows the little guys.

FIGURE 3-7: The knights follow the same general scheme as the other pieces.

FIGURE 3-8: I used flower pots for the pawns.

Playing Chess in Minecraft

A lot of Minecraft players have experimented with playing chess. As a game where your opponent can log in hours or days later and make a move—to play independently—Minecraft seems suited for some sort of turn-based game, though as you probably noticed, the game elements do not readily convert to recognizable chess pieces.

To play, you move your pieces around as you would expect to for chess—only instead of picking up a piece and physically moving it, you must break the block and place those elements in the new position. Needless to say, it's a lot easier to do this in Creative mode, but intrepid Survival players can make use of any element readily broken and replaced.

You'll need a way to signal your opponent that it's his or her turn. Make a simple Redstone Lamp circuit (Figure 3-9) and hit the switch to toggle black or white. When you see the switch has been tripped, just swing over to the board and see what has been moved.

FIGURE 3-9: I use a Redstone Lamp to show which player has the turn.

Place a Sticky Piston block with a Redstone block on the sticky part. Place a Redstone Dust trail leading to one Redstone Lamp and another one leading to a different lamp. When the switch is in its default status (off), one lamp lights up. When the switch is thrown, the other lamp lights up.

In multiplayer mode, it's even simpler. All you have to do is watch as your opponent breaks the piece and places it somewhere else. It's sort of like real chess!

This is my approach, but if you search the Internet you will find other ways players have implemented chess in Minecraft.

Huge Chess

When you scale up enough, even boring cubical Minecraft blocks start looking like specks, and you can build anything, including an absurdly large chess set, like the one seen in Figure 3-10.

FIGURE 3-10: Huge chess pieces allows you to re-create the appearance of the classic game.
CREDIT: YOUTUBE.COM/YAZPANDA

This presents an obvious difficulty: How can playing with cloud-scraping monster chess pieces not be too labor intensive to be viable? Fortunately, Minecraft has the ability to be controlled by Python scripts, allowing you to hypothetically enter the starting and ending coordinates of the chess piece and have a script delete the blocks in the starting square and re-create the piece in the ending square.

Teaching you to program with Python is, however, beyond the scope of what we cover in this book. If you want to learn more about it, search the web for Python and Minecraft together to find online tutorials, videos, and books that will teach you how.

Or Just Download the Texture Pack...

Minecraft texture packs change the appearance of game elements, allowing for fantasy, science fiction, and historical themes. Enterprising Minecrafters have made a chess texture pack in which certain blocks have been given the appearance of chess pieces. In addition to (obviously) playing chess, you could use the elements as decorations for a traditional Minecraft house or build recursive chess pieces out of dozens of smaller chess pieces. Minecraft fan Sibsib92's 3D Chess Sets texture pack (seen in Figure 3-11) swaps in the pieces for carpet squares.

FIGURE 3-11: A texture pack gives ordinary blocks new appearances.

BUILDING A REAL-WORLD CHESS SET

In the real world we have the ability to use mobs in our chess set, because they won't inconveniently explode or wander away. Figure 3-12 shows my set, built out of precisely cut plywood. I'll show you how to build not only this set but one created on a 3D printer.

Make a Glued Wood Set

I created a chess set out of eighth-inch plywood, cut so that the pieces of wood mesh together to form three-dimensional shapes.

FIGURE 3-12: Build this laser-cut chess set.

Parts and Tools

You'll need the following parts and tools to make your chess set:

- Wood: I used Midwest Products' eighth-inch plywood, available from Home Depot, PW001-PY024C. It's very reasonably priced at $3.52 for a 12″×24″ piece.

- Wood glue

- Spray glue—some sort of spray adhesive like 3M Super 77, available in many stores

- Sandpaper

- Spray paint—I used Rust-Oleum gloss black for black; I also suggest Krylon chalkboard paint. I used Rust-Oleum satin white for white.

- Saw—a band saw, coping saw, or computer numerical control (CNC) tool such as a laser cutter

The Pieces

As with any other chess set, my wooden set consists of a king and queen, rooks, bishops, and knights, plus eight pawns per set. Let's examine each piece individually.

The King

The king is Steve, of course, the nickname of the default avatar of the game. How could anyone be the king but you? To give the piece a dynamic flair and to make it taller, I gave the king a Minecraft-style sword, raised overhead. You can see what I created in Figure 3-13.

The Queen

I was originally going to have a different figure for the queen, but I settled on the Enderman (Figure 3-14) mostly because it's the tallest figure—in chess,

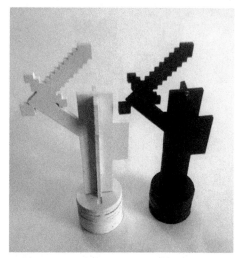

FIGURE 3-13: Steve serves as the king, of course.

the Queen is nearly always the tallest figure, along with the King. In the game, Endermen are the mysterious overlords of the world, so it works for one to serve as queen.

The Rook

The rook is often depicted as a castle of some sort, and I thought about using a nether fortress or village tower for the piece but decided to go with a mob. The Wither, the three-headed skeleton shown in Figure 3-15, is one of the rarest mobs in the game, but it totally deserves to serve as the rook, second in power only to the queen.

The Bishop

For the bishop I went with the Witch, seen in Figure 3-16. These mobs use potions to defeat Steve, but on this board they will serve as bishops, mostly because their pointy hats vaguely resemble a bishop's miter. It's not a perfect analogue, but there are only so many mobs to choose from.

The Knight

You knew the Creeper (Figure 3-17) would show up! Knights jump over other pieces and remind us of the way Creepers can get close and explode before you know it.

FIGURE 3-14: **Mysterious Endermen serve as queens.**

FIGURE 3-15: **Withers are rare monsters in Minecraft.**

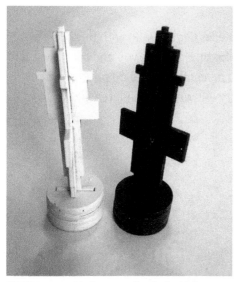

FIGURE 3-16: **Witches standing in for bishops**

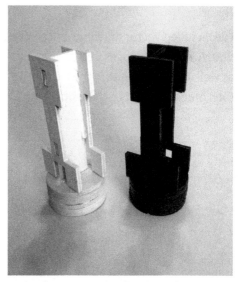

FIGURE 3-17: **Everyone's favorite mob**

The Pawn

Finally, we have the humble pawn, who has the most limited movement of any piece in the game but can swarm the enemy and advance to the opponent's row and become a queen. The two most logical mobs for the pawn would be the skeleton and zombie. I went with the easier of the two, the zombie. You can see what I came up with in Figure 3-18.

Make the Set by Hand...

Those look like some mighty complicated pieces of wood. In this section I'll show you how to make the pieces without the benefit of a laser cutter.

FIGURE 3-18: **Zombie pawns ready for action**

1. Print Off the Designs

I've included vector drawings of the chess pieces (Figure 3-19) with this book's files. A laser cutter uses vector lines as a toolpath. However, you and I can use them as well. Begin by printing the designs at 100 percent on standard printer paper; then glue the paper to the wood. Don't worry—it will sand off later!

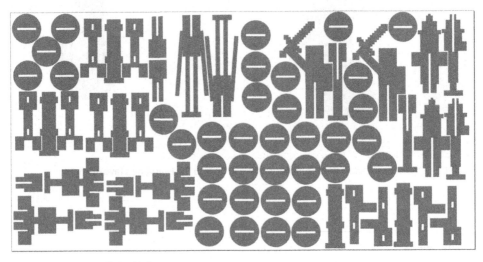

FIGURE 3-19: **Print off the designs.**

You can find the files for these chess pieces online at https://github.com/n1/ MinecraftMakers.

2. Cut Out the Design

Use a coping saw or band saw to cut out the piece. A power tool is likely to yield cleaner lines than a hand saw—but, then, you have less of a chance of cutting off your finger with a hand saw. Whether using hand tools or power tools, always be careful!

Always have adult supervision when using cutting tools.

I designed the pieces so that they can also be cut by laser. This allows for very slick connectors like a mortise and tenon, which is a tab in one piece that connects to a matching hole in the other piece (Figure 3-20). That said, if you're using a saw, simply omit the tabs and holes and just glue the edges together. The pieces are so small they don't *really* need the mortise and tenon to stay together.

When you're done cutting, sand off the paper.

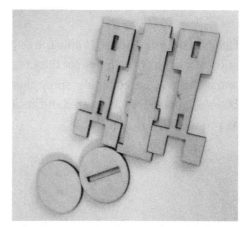

FIGURE 3-20: **A mortise and tenon**

3. Glue the Piece

Glue the various elements together to form the piece. Figure 3-21 shows me gluing a queen together.

4. Attach the Base

I used circular bases (Figure 3-22) for my chess pieces, even though they're sort of noncanonical in block-crazy Minecraft. If you're sawing your pieces rather than using a laser cutter, you might want to simply use square-cut wood. Alternatively, you could get a length of 1.5″ dowel and cut off slices to use as bases, with lengths differing depending on the importance of the piece.

As with the mortise and tenon, you can omit the slots and simply glue the chess pieces directly to the base.

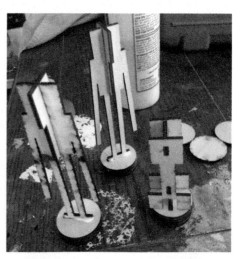

FIGURE 3-21: **Just glue it.**

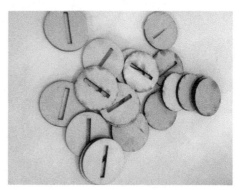

FIGURE 3-22: **Give each piece a base.**

5. Paint

Finally, paint your pieces. I know the temptation is to decorate them in game-authentic colors (e.g., green for the Creeper knight), but I chose the classic black and white look. I used regular spray paint and simply set the pieces down on cardboard (Figure 3-23) and sprayed the heck out of them. Feel free to paint your pieces as you see fit!

FIGURE 3-23: **Paint the figures.**

...or Laser-Cut It

Figure 3-24 shows a version of my set straight from the CNC machine.

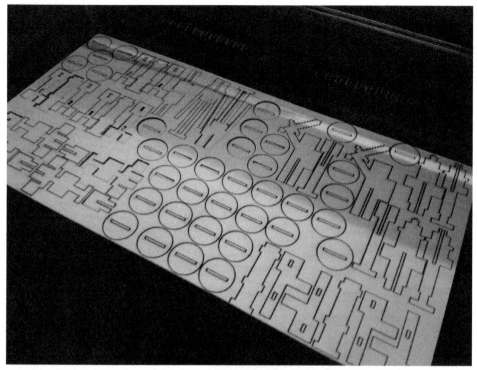

FIGURE 3-24: **Chess pieces in pieces**

The laser cutter is my favorite tool. It moves on X and Y axes to cut precise shapes in wood and plastic. Laser cutters are not something every maker can afford, or would even want in their home workshop. Before you give up on making the set this way, however, here are some options to consider:

Local Services: If you're close to a city, you'll likely find laser-cutting services that could output your project for a fee. You'll pay for laser time as well as the cost of materials.

Remote Services: You'll find countless laser-cutting services available on the Internet, with a place to upload your files and select materials. You'll pay for shipping and handling on top of laser time and materials, of course.

Schools and Maker Spaces: You'd be surprised how many institutions nearby have equipment you could use for free (or cheap). Some libraries now contain "maker spaces" with 3D printers, CNC mills, and laser cutters available for public use. Community colleges typically have such a facility for use by students. Finally, there are independent organizations, sometimes called *hackerspaces*, that are warehouses filled with tools and computers for use by members. My hackerspace charges $55 a month in dues and $5 an hour to use the laser, plus you buy your own materials. You'd be surprised what resources you can find for not much money.

Painting and Decorating the Set

As mentioned earlier, I prefer the classic black and white look of chess sets, with the color not representing anything specific on the piece. For that reason, the idea of painting the pieces to match the mob didn't interest me much. That said, you can paint your set any way you want.

I've been using a lovely matte chalkboard paint on my projects (specified in the parts list) and thought it would be perfect for the black set. At the last minute, however, I swapped in standard glossy black (Figure 3-25) and it worked great. The white set I painted a basic satin white.

Once you're done painting, you may want to consider gluing a disc of felt to the bottom of each piece to give it a smooth delivery.

FIGURE 3-25: **Painting the chess set**

Make a 3D Printed Chess Set

3D printers typically manufacture items from various kinds of plastic filament. 3D models fed into the printer tell it what to do. If you have access to a 3D printer, it's a cinch to assemble a Minecraft-themed chess set because so many people have created models from the game and posted them online. In fact, all of your work has been done for you because fans of the game have assembled their own sets.

The following are examples of printable Minecraft chess pieces gleaned from various sources on the web. Simply searching for "3D printed chess" should give you plenty of hits, though you might have better luck finding what you want on websites like https://www.thingiverse.com/ that collect 3D-printed designs anyone can download.

Creeper

Thingiverse user FuelCell250 designed this Creeper model (seen in Figure 3-26) as part of his Minecraft Chess Set (#143991), which uses Slimes as pawns, among other solutions.

Enderman

One thing I like about this Enderman (Figure 3-27) is that it has ball-and-socket arm joints, meaning you could move them around if you wanted. I found it on the Microsoft corporate page on Thingiverse, labeled as Thing #452105.

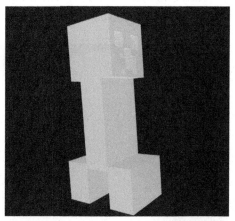

FIGURE 3-26: **This Creeper works perfectly as a chess piece.**

Ghast

Thingiverse user jezza770's chess set (#577412) includes a Ghast piece. I found the choice a little eyebrow-raising because it's also physically huge and bigger than most other mobs, and scaling it down looks a little odd.

FIGURE 3-27: **Make your Enderman with posable arms.**

However, you can take the Ghast (Figure 3-28) from the set and use it for whatever piece you want, or even go back to the original—jezza770's Ghast is a remix of another piece on Thingiverse, #86708.

Skeleton

Thingiverse user giufini's skeleton (#678131) was not specifically intended to be a chess piece—at least there's nothing on the page—but it's posed

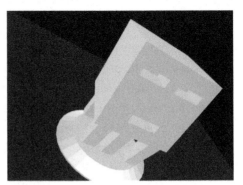

FIGURE 3-28: The Ghast piece is a remix of another artist's creation.

perfectly and even has a base. The model comes in two parts—the main Skeleton (Figure 3-29), and you can also print up a Minecraft bow for it to hold.

FIGURE 3-29: This Skeleton model also comes with a bow.

Slime

FuelCell250's chess set (mentioned earlier) uses Slimes for pawns, as seen in Figure 3-30.

Spider

Thingiverse user Jeremy8077 build 3D-printable versions of Withers and Spiders (#495956). He intended the Spiders to serve as pawns, and in Figure 3-31 you can see he has the file set to print eight at once.

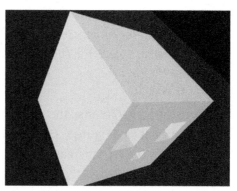

FIGURE 3-30: **Need some Slime?**

FIGURE 3-31: **Like Spiders? Make them your chess pawns.**

Steve/Zombie

Another offering of the Minecraft page on Thingiverse, the Steve figure (seen in Figure 3-32) also serves as a Zombie. You can print it with articulated arms and head if you want. Search for Thing #452140.

Villager/Witch

Similar to the Steve/Zombie, the Villager also doubles as the Witch, with the addition of a hat (see Figure 3-33). Thingiverse user martialmedia has a version of the Villager (#403897), whereas user camandrula remixed Microsoft's Steve into a Villager and Witch (#1482477) including a separately downloadable Witch hat that can be added to any Villager figure.

FIGURE 3-32: Microsoft shares this Steve figure, which can double as a Zombie.

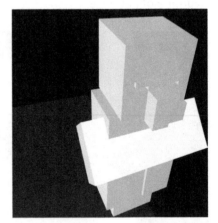

FIGURE 3-33: Want to turn a Villager into a Witch? Just add a hat.

Wither

Another powerful critter from the game, the Wither (Figure 3-34) makes a great chess piece. Thingiverse user LEGOTNT made a version of the Wither (#1298538) that fits the bill.

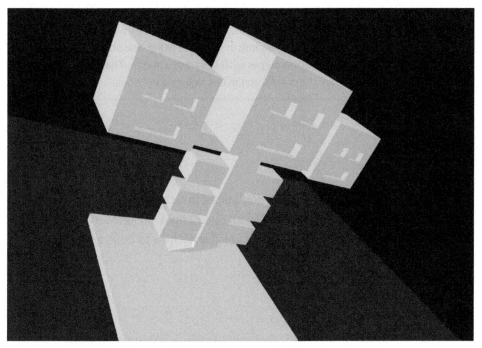

FIGURE 3-34: The Wither is a powerful mob in the game.

Wolf

Minecraft Wolves are not powerful mobs, but they are omnipresent in the game, and many players take pains to domesticate them. Evil-Techy made the Wolf shown in Figure 3-35, downloadable at Thing #328399.

If you don't own a 3D printer, don't worry. As is the case with laser cutters and other CNC machines, you can find 3D printing services online. You will also find that 3D printers are often available at local schools, libraries, and makerspaces.

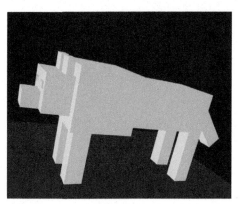

FIGURE 3-35: Wolves aren't tough mobs, but many players love them.

As with the wooden chess set, you have the option to make the pieces any color you want, whether to conform to the game or for some other reason. Traditionally the set consists of black and white pieces with squares to match. That said, I've seen some really cool full-color chess sets, so I'm not saying don't do it.

SUMMARY

Chess sets, both virtual and physical, dominated this chapter. But let's switch gears back to the classic block. In Chapter 4 you'll build a light-up Redstone Ore block that will really tie the room together, and you'll learn how to build a basic LED circuit.

Advanced Projects

LED-Lit Minecraft Block

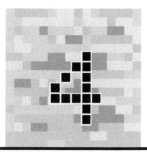

In this chapter, you'll continue to explore ways to re-create the iconic Minecraft block, making a larger, wooden version decorated with stenciled patterns. We'll begin with a painted block that looks cool but doesn't do anything, before leveling up with a light-up version of the Redstone Ore block, shown in Figure 4-1. Follow along to see how to build both versions.

FIGURE 4-1: Make your own LED-lit Redstone Ore block!

MAKING A WOODEN MINECRAFT BLOCK

Before we work with LEDs, let's make a simple wooden cube, a block consisting of six-inch panels of plywood (Figure 4-2) glued together to form a cube. I used a laser cutter to make my block, but it's a high-end tool many people can't access, so I'll also show you how to build your block with commonplace hand and power tools.

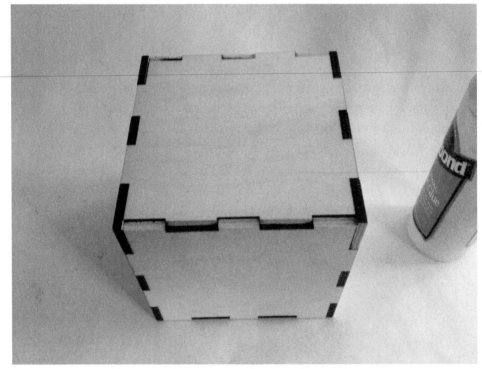

FIGURE 4-2: **Make a simple wooden block.**

Making the Plywood Block on a Saw

Making a six-inch block out of pieces of plywood presents much more of a challenge than you might expect. I will show you two ways to build it: by hand and with a laser cutter.

The hand-built block consists of six pieces of wood glued together to make a box shape. It can be surprisingly difficult to get a cube that looks visually perfect. You'll want to measure carefully to ensure the project looks right.

There is also the matter of the holes in the wood (Figure 4-3), through which the LED will shine and remind us of Redstone Ore blocks. It's *possible* to cut them by hand and I'll show you how, but I chose to start simple. Accordingly, the hand-cut cube won't have holes or light up, and the red color will be made with a stencil and spray paint.

FIGURE 4-3: **The laser-cut cube allows for light to shine through.**

Parts List

You'll need just a few things to build your block:

- Quarter-inch or ⅜″ plywood— I often use a great 12″ × 24″ birch plywood from Home Depot, PW002-PY024C. However, if you're cutting the wood with a saw, you can probably find cheaper stuff. I found a piece of scrap ⅜″ plywood for free.

- Saw—a table saw ideally, but a band saw or circular saw might work as well. You'll also need a jigsaw or coping saw for cutting the ore holes.

- Wood glue

- Clamps

- Printer

- Spray adhesive such as 3M Super 77

Steps—Flat-Sided Method

If you don't have access to computer-guided machinery to build the six-inch plywood block, you'd do best to forget the finger joints and just use flat sides, relying on glue and nails to keep it together.

1. Cut Out Wood

Cut the six pieces of plywood as shown in Figure 4-4A; two are 6″×6″ in size and will serve as the top and bottom of the block; the sides, front, and back must be adjusted based on the thickness of the wood. You should double-check the thickness of the stock you're using. Some kinds of wood have a nominal width and an actual width. My nominally quarter-inch plywood was actually 0.236″. If I size my cuts based on 0.25″, my block might not be a cube.

However, for the sake of simplicity, let's pretend the stock thickness is exactly 0.25″. The height of the sides is reduced by 0.5″ (0.25× 2) to account for the thickness of the top and bottom.

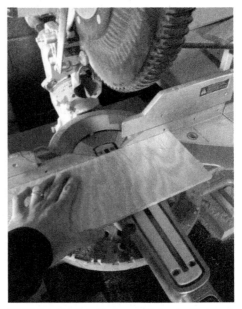

FIGURE 4-4A: Cut six pieces of plywood to form a 6″ cube.

In addition, two of the sides' lengths are reduced by a similar amount. Figure 4-4B shows how to size each piece.

top/bottom
6x6

left/right
6x5.5

front/back
5.5x5.5

FIGURE 4-4B: Patterns for cutting with a saw

2. Glue One Corner

Take two of the sides, one 6″ long and the other 5.528″ (okay, 5.5″ will be fine), and glue them together, clamping as needed. Make sure to keep it as square as possible, because after it is glued and clamped, it won't want to be adjusted. The best solution I found was to add a third panel, as seen in Figure 4-5.

3. Finish the Square

Add the other two sides (Figure 4-6) and then glue them together.

FIGURE 4-5: Glue and clamp one corner of the block.

4. Add the Top

Finally, add the top to complete the cube, as shown in Figure 4-7. You may want to leave the top loose and use it for storage. If not, I suggest adding a couple of penny nails to each glued edge to keep it in place, though my block used no nails and is holding together nicely.

FIGURE 4-6: Finish the square by adding the other two sides.

FIGURE 4-7: Finish the block by adding the top and bottom.

Steps—Toothed Method

If you are a bold soul and want to tackle the toothed, light-up version of the Redstone Ore block with hand and power tools, follow these steps.

1. Print Off Designs

You can find the 6″ toothed block design with the files accompanying this book, https://github.com/n1/MinecraftMakers. Print off each side at 100 percent on standard printer paper (Figure 4-8).

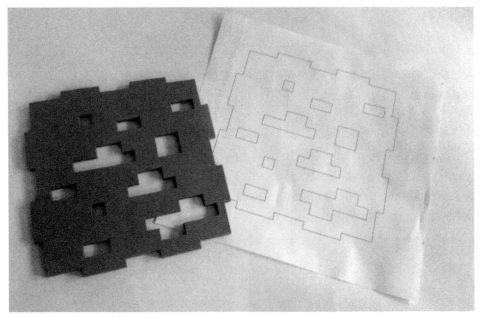

FIGURE 4-8: **Print off the designs.**

2. Adhere to Plywood

Use glue—I suggest spray adhesive like 3M Super 77—to attach the design to the plywood. Figure 4-9 shows the design in place.

FIGURE 4-9: **Glue the design to plywood.**

3. Cut Through the Design

Use a saw to cut through the design. When each part is done, sand off the old design. Figure 4-10 shows me in mid-cut.

4. Cut Ore Holes

To cut the ore holes, first drill them with a standard drill (Figure 4-11) and then clean them up with a jigsaw or coping saw.

5. Glue and Clamp

Finish the block as you did the previous one. You'll definitely want to leave one side unglued so you can add the LED and battery pack later.

FIGURE 4-10: **Cut through the design.**

FIGURE 4-11: **Drill through the ore holes to make room for a jigsaw blade.**

Making the Block with a Laser Cutter

Far easier than either of the preceding methods, laser cutting makes precise cuts and it's therefore easier to cut out the finger joints. The cutter essentially is an industrial laser in a cabinet, with mirrors mounted on motorized tracks. It can cut exact shapes out of plywood, acrylic, and other materials, making it ideal for assemblies like, well, boxes.

It costs a lot of money, as you might expect. However, you'd be surprised how many laser cutters may be found in your community, and access to them can often be had for little money. For instance, your local makerspace, tool library, or hackerspace may have one. Community colleges and tech schools also have them. Finally, you can send out your designs to services like Ponoko (https://www.ponoko.com), which can output your files in a variety of materials and ship them back to you.

1. Open the Design in InkScape (or Wherever…)

There are too many different types of laser cutting software for me to offer a specific guide to what happens next, but on the machine I use, you open up the design in a software program called InkScape (Figure 4-12) and "print" the design through

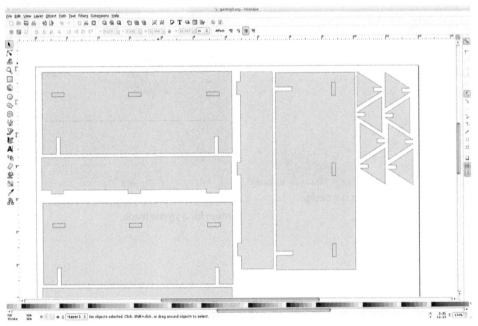

FIGURE 4-12: Open the file in InkScape.

the Print dialog. Instead of going to a printer, however, the command activates laser cutting software. From the dialog, you can adjust the laser's speed and power. Another setting you may encounter is the distance between the laser's emitter and the material. All of these are factors that will differ depending on the make and model of your laser and the sort of material you're cutting.

2. Laser Out the Parts

Having entered the right settings, place the material on the bed of the laser cutter and get to laserin'. Figure 4-13 shows the sides of the block, freshly cut and ready for assembly and painting.

3. Assemble the Parts

To assemble the block, simply piece together the parts—note that the top and bottom are different than the four sides—and then glue. If necessary, clamp as shown in Figure 4-14, but oftentimes a structure like this will fit together with friction and won't need clamping. Again, leave one side unglued so you can put in the LED later on.

FIGURE 4-13: **Laser out the sides.**

FIGURE 4-14: **Glue the sides together.**

Painting the Block

Regardless of which block you build, you'll still need to paint it. Given the mechanical precision of the blocks' pattern, it's easiest to use stencils (Figure 4-15) to decorate it. In this section I'll show you how to cut stencils to decorate your blocks.

Parts

Making stencils is pretty easy, and the process requires only a few parts:

- Printer
- Spray glue like 3M Super 77
- Posterboard or heavier
- X-Acto knives

Steps

Follow these steps to cut the stencils.

1. Print, Glue, and Cut the Stencils

You're a pro at this by now. Print off the stencil patterns—there is one for light gray, one for dark gray, and an optional ore stencil for a third color if your block won't light up. Adhere the pages to posterboard, and then use an X-Acto knife to cut out the design. Leave plenty of room along the edges—at least 1″ to keep your spray paint off areas it's not supposed to be. Figure 4-16 shows the completed stencils.

FIGURE 4-15: **Cut stencils to decorate your block.**

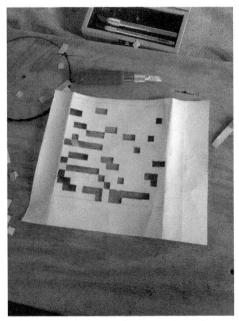

FIGURE 4-16: **Print and cut out the stencils.**

2. Paint the Background Color

Begin by painting the background color. I used Rust-Oleum "granite" gray for mine.

3. Apply the Stencils

Position the light gray stencil on the block very carefully; then spray it. I used a little silver paint in place of light gray (Figure 4-17) because I didn't have any. When that's dry, apply the gray stencil and then paint that color.

FIGURE 4-17: **Apply the light gray stencil.**

4. Finish the Paint

If your block won't be illuminated, apply the ore stencil and paint. Decorate each side with the various stencils. You may want to save one side until the very end, or simply leave the bottom unpainted. Figure 4-18 shows the completed block.

FIGURE 4-18: **Use the ore stencil to paint the ore pattern.**

Lighting the Block

Next, let's make that Redstone Ore glow. We'll add an LED and battery pack to the inside, with red construction paper giving the glow the requisite ruby color (Figure 4-19).

Parts List

You'll need the following parts to light up the block:

- LED—Super Bright White, Spark-Fun P/N #531

- Battery pack with barrel jack and switch (e.g., Adafruit P/N 67) or a 9V DC power supply (SparkFun P/N 298)

- DC power adapter such as Spark-Fun P/N 10288

- Wires—SparkFun sells a wire assortment, P.N 11367

- Resistor—330-ohm resistors will do the job; SparkFun P/N 11507

- Red construction paper or some other kind of paper

- Hot glue

FIGURE 4-19: **Make your block light up!**

Steps

Follow these steps to finish the project.

1. Glue in the Paper

Spray the inside of the cube with spray adhesive and apply the pieces of paper, used to diffuse the light coming from inside. If you're using a bright white LED, you may want to go with red construction paper, whereas white paper (like the printer paper seen in Figure 4-20) works with a red LED.

FIGURE 4-20: **Glue in the paper.**

2. Attach the Power Supply

Use small wood screws or hot glue to attach the battery pack to the inside of the block. For added points, position the battery pack so that its switch can be manipulated through one of the ore holes. Alternatively, you could use a 9V power supply (Figure 4-21) and never run out of batteries.

FIGURE 4-21: The 9V power supply plugs right into the wall.

3. Connect the Adapter

The battery pack I chose has a barrel plug, so we'll need an adapter to attach it to wires. Just plug it in! Figure 4-22 shows a rendering of the adapter.

FIGURE 4-22: The DC adapter connects the power supply to a circuit.

4. Add the Resistor

Attach one leg of the resistor to the adapter's positive lead, as shown in Figure 4-23. This protects the LED from getting too much voltage.

FIGURE 4-23: Attach one leg of the resistor to the adapter.

5. Add the LED

Attach the long lead of the LED to the free end of the resistor. Just twist the ends together for now, making sure they remain in contact. Figure 4-24 shows the LED in place.

6. Close the Circuit

The shorter lead of the LED attaches to the ground (–) pin of the adapter, completing the circuit. Figure 4-25 shows the final wiring diagram.

FIGURE 4-24: **Add the LED.**

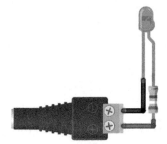

FIGURE 4-25: **Close the circuit.**

7. Close the Top and Light It Up

Once you have the battery pack and LED in place, it's time to see the results of your hard work. Figure 4-26 shows the completed project.

FIGURE 4-26: **Light it up.**

SUMMARY

In this chapter you did it all: simple blocks, complicated blocks, blocks that light up. But we're not yet done with the Minecraft block. In Chapter 5, you'll build your own full-sized light fixture that plays homage to Redstone Lamp blocks.

Redstone Lamp

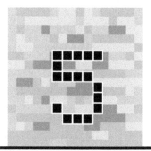

The next project takes our light-up block techniques to the next level. This time we'll make a larger assembly that works as a lamp or chandelier, running off house current and very much usable for illumination. You can see what I came up with in Figure 5-1.

We'll begin by designing the lamp in-game. As I mentioned earlier, one of the advantages of re-creating a game element is that you can design it using the game itself. I'll also guide you through buying the light-up element and fabricating the structure that will support it.

FIGURE 5-1: My Redstone Lamp, ensconced in my house

BUILD A REDSTONE LAMP

Before you can begin building your lamp, you must first determine its dimensions. The best way involves designing the lamp in-game.

Design Your Chandelier In-Game

In a sense, Minecraft works like a real-world building set like LEGO or K'Nex in that you have a limited array of parts with which to build. Why not just prototype your light fixture in the game, get it looking the way you want it, and then translate it?

Let's begin by taking into consideration what sort of light you want to build. You can choose among countless configurations, such as a table, floor, or pendant lamp. This will be dictated by your own needs. For me, I chose a table lamp because I needed an accent lamp for my bedroom.

Then, you'll hop into Minecraft's Creative mode and build a couple iterations of designs, allowing you to come up with the final blueprints for the physical build.

Steps

Follow these steps to build your light fixture.

1. Begin with a Real-World Light Fixture

The smart move is to design your lamp to go with a specific light fixture product rather than try to find a fixture to match your perfect design. Without any specific needs in terms of configuration, I chose a classic approach with a socket with a turn-switch on it, a cord, and hardware to attach it all to the enclosure.

You'll find many prewired lighting products out there, with any option you'd need: multiple sockets, dimmer controls, or extra-long cords, any of which could be useful depending on your project. You'll sometimes see these marketed as "lamp kits."

Feel free to think outside of the box, too. LED strips are also an option, such as the strips found in vehicle customizations. I picked up some holiday lights featuring an "icicle" configuration with short vertical strands hanging off a longer horizontal string. For more of an accent lamp, holiday lights may be an option.

That being said, I wanted a small lamp for a set of shelves in my bedroom, so I went with a classic socket (Figure 5-2) found everywhere.

Here are some factors to keep in mind when choosing *your* light fixture:

- Lamp use: Will you need to read/see with the lamp or is its purpose just to look cool?

- Bulb types: I chose an attractive LED bulb but also strongly considered getting a "smart" bulb that can be controlled with a remote control or phone app.

- Wiring distances: How long between the socket and the first light? If there is a dimmer, where is it positioned along the power cord? These are all important because you want the finished lamp to be the right distance away from the outlet.

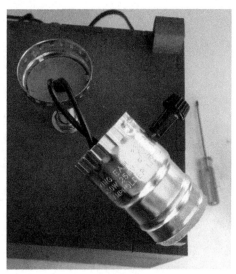

FIGURE 5-2: **Choose a light fixture.**

- Number of bulbs: Depending on how huge your fixture will be, it may have multiple sockets.

- Configuration: There are some classic configurations like pendant lights and table lights, light strips, and wall sconces.

- Hardware: How does the fixture attach to the lamp's body? Threaded tubes, like I use in the project, may be found in any number of lengths, and it's fairly standard in the industry.

- Switching: Many products have a built-in switch or dimmer, but worst-case scenario, you can always plug and unplug the lamp to turn it on and off.

2. Build Your First Iteration

Keeping the basic configuration in mind, go into Minecraft in Creative mode and begin throwing blocks around. If you're building a pendant light, you'll need to imagine how it will connect to the ceiling. A floor lamp will need a long neck. And how big of a shade will you create? Figure 5-3 shows an initial concept for my lamp, which features more of a spread-out and somewhat ambitious design.

FIGURE 5-3: **Build a light in Minecraft.**

3. Rebuild Your Design

Your first idea may not be the best one. It doesn't hurt to build one or more subsequent iterations, and perhaps you'll discover something new and better—or maybe that first idea proves to be the best one. Figure 5-4 shows more of a classic table lamp, though I found the barbell structure rather inelegant.

4. Settle On a Design

Having explored the possibilities, it's time to settle on a design. I chose a simple three-block stack for my table lamp, as shown in Figure 5-5. It eliminates the annoying barbell look while providing the maximum amount of light.

FIGURE 5-4: **Rebuild your design.**

FIGURE 5-5: **My final design involves three blocks.**

5. Sketch It in the Real World (IRL)

The final step to designing the lamp is to sketch it (Figure 5-6) in order to determine dimensions. I decided on a 6″×6″ footprint, making the lamp 18″ tall. I chose these mostly based on the dimensions of the bookshelf on which the lamp will be placed, though it didn't hurt that I had already made 6″ blocks in the previous chapter, so I could use them to visualize how the final lamp would look.

6. Translate the Drawing Into a Design

I used Inkscape to create each panel of the shade and base, with 11 total

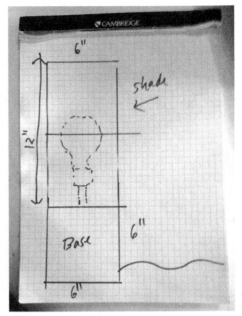

FIGURE 5-6: **Sketch out your lamp design.**

boards. Figure 5-7 shows what I designed in Inkscape, and you can download this file yourself (https://github.com/n1/MinecraftMakers) and use it however you want. Lacking computer controlled tools, you can still use the design by gluing it to a board and cutting it out.

FIGURE 5-7: **Create blueprints in Inkscape.**

> Inkscape is a free, open source drawing program that you can download here: https://inkscape.org.

Build the Physical Lamp

With the design established, it's time to work on the real-world lamp.

Parts and Tools

None of these supplies should surprise...

- Light set—I went with a fairly traditional configuration, Westinghouse products found at Home Depot:
    - 2.5″ socket with turn switch, P/N 70403
    - 8′ cord, P/N 70101
    - Nuts and washers set, P/N 70628
    - Zinc-plated nipples, P/N 70150
- Plywood—I've had good results with ⅛″ plywood and ¼″ plywood, used for previous projects in this book, and that are available from your local home improvement store.
- Scrap wood—1×4 pine boards will work, cut to size
- Table saw
- Drill and bits
- Jigsaw or coping saw
- Sandpaper
- Parchment
- Spray paint: I used ordinary spray paint, bronze colored.
- Spray adhesive like 3M Super 77

Steps

Enough designing; let's make this thing!

7. Cut the Shade Panels

Let's begin with the shade. Spray-glue the design to a piece of wood. I chose ⅛″ plywood but ¼″ will work too if you change the depth of the finger joints. Use a table saw to trim the edges to the boundaries indicated on the design. To cut the interior parts, drill a hole (Figure 5-8) and pass the jigsaw blade through the hole and make your cuts.

A handheld coping saw works in much the same away, except that you have to remove the blade from the saw handle in order to pass it through the hole. Simply reattach the blade and make your cuts.

FIGURE 5-8: Cut the shade panels.

8. Glue the Sides

Using ¼″ sticks of scrap wood at the join, glue the panels together. Figure 5-9 shows all the panels in place.

9. Cut the Base Boards

Cut the panels for the base. This looks remarkably like the non-lighting block (Figure 5-10) you built in in Chapter 3. It's a 6″×6″×6″ cube. I made mine out of ¼″ plywood for greater stability, though the ⅛″ stuff is pretty solid as well.

Repeat the process where you print out the design and glue it to wood. Use

FIGURE 5-9: Glue the other panels of the shade.

a chop saw or table saw to trim off the excess, before cutting out the finger joints with a band saw or jigsaw. Or you can simply build a box out of boards as I did in Chapter 3.

Regardless of which technique you employ, be sure to leave one side unglued so you can add the electrical components. While you're at it, drill a ⅜″ hole for the threaded tube in the center of the top and a ¼″ hole in the backside through which the electrical cord will pass.

10. Glue the Base

As expected, glue the panels of plywood together. You may want to secure the bottom with screws so you can get access to the lamp guts. While you're at it, add a couple of blocks of scrap wood (Figure 5-11) to help keep the shade in place. Position four pieces of scrap while the shade is in place to ensure they're set correctly. These will keep the shade from falling off.

FIGURE 5-10: **Cut panels for the base.**

Painting and Decorating the Lamp

When the glue is dry, paint the lamp. I used the bronze and brown spray paint specified in the parts list. Then I glued sheets of parchment to help diffuse the lamp.

11. Paint the Shade

I used my bronze paint to spray the shade, as seen in Figure 5-12. It's not a game-authentic color—Redstone blocks have more black in them—but I wanted something that reflected the warm metallic colors in the room. I painted the base a generic brown, not wanting to attract attention to it.

FIGURE 5-11: **Glue the base.**

12. Glue in the Parchment

Spray the inside of the shade with Super 77 and add sheets of parchment to cover the holes on all five sides. Actually, any glue will do; I used regular white glue myself, and it seemed to work fine. Figure 5-13 shows the parchment going in.

Wiring the Socket

Once the paint's dry, it's time to add the guts of the lamp: the socket, wires, and hardware.

FIGURE 5-12: **Paint the shade a bronze color.**

13. Install the Threaded Pipe

Electrical lights use a threaded ⅜″ pipe onto which you attach the socket and to accommodate the wires. I passed the nipple through the hole and secured it at both ends with washers and nuts. Figure 5-14 shows the pipe in place.

FIGURE 5-13: **Add parchment sheets.**

FIGURE 5-14: **The threaded pipe installed**

14. Add the Power Cord

Pass the power cord through the ¼″ hole in the lamp back. Draw it up and through the threaded pipe as well as the bottom part of the socket, as shown in Figure 5-15. The latter screws onto the pipe and is tightened with a set screw.

FIGURE 5-15: **Add the power cord.**

15. Tie an Underwriter's Knot

Before we can attach the cord to the socket, we need to tie an under-writer's knot (see Figure 5-16). This reduces the chance that yanking on the cord will disconnect a wire. If you can't see how to make such a knot in the photo, just Google it.

16. Wire Up the Socket

One of the wires has ribbing along one side, and one does not. The ribbed wire is the ground wire (–), whereas the unadorned wire is lead (+). Remove the socket from its brass enclosure as well as the cardboard sleeve inside, allowing you to get at the screw terminals you'll use to secure the wires. Figure 5-17 shows the wires in place.

FIGURE 5-16: **The underwriter's knot reduces the chance of a wire getting pulled out.**

17. Close Up the Socket

Having completed the wiring, finish the project by closing up the socket again.

FIGURE 5-17: **Wire up the socket.**

Add a light bulb and replace the shade. You're done! Figure 5-18 shows another beauty shot of the completed lamp.

FIGURE 5-18: **The Redstone Lamp project, all lit up**

SUMMARY

In this chapter, you built a lamp, guiding the project through its development in Minecraft, to designing the enclosure and transferring it onto wood, to wiring up the final creation. In Chapter 6, you'll continue your mastery of light-up blocks by creating a Minecraft-inspired chess board to go with the set you built earlier in the book.

Light-Up Chess Board

In Chapter 3 you built your own Minecraft-themed chess set. All you need now is a board to go with it. In this chapter, you'll assemble a chess board mostly out of wood, using ordinary woodshop tools. For added pizzazz you'll add a string of holiday lights that will make the white squares light up, as well as an acrylic sheet for the top. Figure 6-1 shows the final project.

FIGURE 6-1: The Minecraft chess board ready for play.

BUILDING A MINECRAFT CHESS BOARD

To build the board, you'll need to prototype your design in-game, and then move to the woodshop to create the project.

Prototyping the Board in Minecraft

You can only modify the classic board so much. It's an 8×8 grid with alternating black and white squares. So, how can you make it your own?

Once again, I returned to the game to build virtual prototypes of my project and filled up my Creative world with a plethora of chess boards. I began with the classic look, using Coal and Marble blocks initially. However, I knew I wanted the white squares to light up, and I didn't want to be blinded. I tried out some Sea Lantern blocks (Figure 6-2), but the overall aesthetic seemed very cold and icy.

FIGURE 6-2: The chess board with Sea Lantern blocks

For my second iteration I built a chess board out of Glowstone (Figure 6-3) and I liked it a lot. This resembles the board I built for Chapter 3, but this one was built on plains instead of a mountaintop. It's basic, but I can't think of any other elements that does a better job of evoking the classic set. I decided this was the approach I wanted to take toward building my real-world board.

FIGURE 6-3: **Swapping in Glowstone**

Building the Board

Having settled on a design, it's time to start building. The black squares are blocks of wood, and the white squares are parchment squares printed with a Glowstone block pattern. The top is covered with an acrylic sheet, and lighting will be provided by a string of holiday lights.

Parts and Tools

Gather together the following parts and tools:

- Plywood sheet: The size you want your board to be; I made my 16″×16″.
- Wood—1.5″–2″ thick, based on how thick you want your board to be.
- Holiday lights: Use your favorite string of holiday lights, around 15′ in length with lights every 4–5 inches.
- Résumé paper or other printable parchment
- Drill press
- Table saw

Building Steps

Having assembled everything you need, it's time to start building:

1. Cut the Base

Cut a 16″×16″ piece of plywood. It can just be a random piece of scrap wood, like the one seen in Figure 6-4. This board can be practically anything, because it will be covered up by other elements. Keep in mind that the plywood adds to the overall thickness of the board.

2. Draw Guides

Draw a grid (Figure 6-5) corresponding with the board pattern. This will help guide the blocks into position.

FIGURE 6-4: **Cut a piece of plywood for the base.**

3. Cut the Blocks

Cut thirty-two 2″×2″ blocks. In terms of thickness, these blocks can be anything—from an old 2×4 lying around, for instance. It just needs to be thick enough to fit the lights through it—I suggest at least 1.5″. Figure 6-6 shows my stack of blocks.

FIGURE 6-5: Draw guides on the base.

FIGURE 6-6: Cut the wood into 2″×2″ blocks.

4. Drill the Blocks

In each block, drill a hole wide enough to admit your strand of lights. It's vital to secure the wood so that it doesn't twist free and spin on the bit. Figure 6-7 shows a no-spin jig I built that makes each block the same.

I drilled each block straight through, but I had hoped to make a right-angle hole by drilling halfway through on one side, then turning the wood 90 degrees and drilling halfway through there as well. However, the medium-density fiberboard (MDF) I used was too flimsy and those attempts ruined the block. You might have better luck with thicker material or by swapping in some hardwood.

Another question to consider is, would even a 1″ hole admit your light string? Many holiday lights are meant to be daisy-chained, so there is an electrical socket on the end that might provide difficult to thread through a hole. One solution might be to drill the holes, cut through the hole to make a half-circle, and then glue the wiring directly to the board.

Once you've drilled the blocks (Figure 6-8), you're ready to paint them.

5. Paint the Blocks

Spray the sides of the squares white, ideally avoiding spraying the tops. This step adds a little reflection to make the white squares light up more.

FIGURE 6-7: **Secure the wood blocks for drilling.**

FIGURE 6-8: **Drilled blocks**

Once the white sides are done, group the blocks together (Figure 6-9) and paint the tops black. Although the parchment will be covering up the black squares with black printing, the spray paint won't hurt.

6. Secure the Blocks

Go through and glue each block to the board, following along with the grid you drew. Figure 6-10 shows the board with the squares glued. Be sure you know how you'll attach the lights before you glue the blocks.

7. Thread the Lights Through

Position the squares on the board with the holes all pointing in the same direction. Thread the lights through; make sure that a light is in each white square (see Figure 6-11).

FIGURE 6-9: **Painting the blocks**

FIGURE 6-10: **Glue the squares.**

FIGURE 6-11: **Thread the lights through the squares.**

8. Install the Edges

Add strips of wood or molding to the sides, and make sure it's wide enough to cover not only the height of the squares but the thickness of the base and the thickness of the acrylic playing surface that will cover the top. Figure 6-12 shows the edge pieces being installed. When adding the edges, be sure to allow for the lights' power cord. The easiest way to do so is to thread it through where the corners meet.

FIGURE 6-12: **Add the edges.**

9. Print the Parchment Pages

Print the top design (you can find it among the downloads at github.com/n1) onto sheets of résumé paper. Trim the edges (Figure 6-13) and tape the pages into a 16″×16″ sheet corresponding with the surface of the table.

10. Apply the Printed Sheet

Lay the printed sheet (Figure 6-14) over the top of the blocks, with the black squares obviously sitting on the wooden blocks and the white squares over the lights. Figure 6-14 shows how it should look. Remember to keep a white square in the lower-left corner and you're set!

The board is nearly finished. Put a 16″×16″ sheet of acrylic or glass on top of the parchment sheet. If the board isn't going to be moved, you might be able to get away with relying on gravity to keep it in place. Otherwise, glue strips of wood to the edges to keep the pane in place.

FIGURE 6-13: Tape the pieces of résumé paper together to form the surface.

FIGURE 6-14: Tape the printed pages into a single large sheet.

SUMMARY

In this chapter you made a chess board (Figure 6-15) to match the pieces you built in Chapter 3. Care for a game?

FIGURE 6-15: It's time to play some chess!

PART 3

Arduino Projects

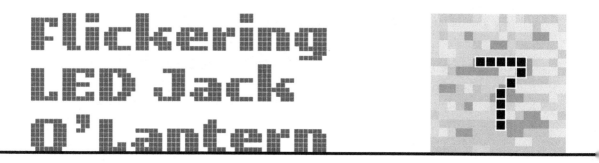

Flickering LED Jack O'Lantern

The next project continues with the theme of light-up Minecraft re-creations. You're going to build the ultimate Minecraft Jack O'Lantern to frighten Creepers, Zombies, and assorted trick-or-treaters. The project consists of a pumpkin (Figure 7-1) made out of orange corrugated plastic (Coroplast), painted to match the game element and given an Arduino-controlled LED module that creates a flickering flame effect without having to rely on actual flame. That's a lot to learn, so let's get started!

FIGURE 7-1: The Jack O'Lantern is sure to scare off mobs and kids.

MINECRAFT JACK O'LANTERN

The first part of the build involves creating the Coroplast cube. Let's begin by researching how it should look by once again taking our design eyes into the video game.

Design It

The Jack O'Lantern has a different design for the top than for the sides. Figure 7-2 shows the game element. For my needs I'm assuming a 1´ cube, making each square of the design 0.75˝ in real-world measurements. Of course, blocks are considered one meter in size, so there's lots of room to move up if you want to make a bigger splash.

FIGURE 7-2: The Minecraft Jack O'Lantern

Build It

Having designed the Jack O'Lantern, it's time to make it. But first, you'll need to gather together the following.

Parts and Tools

You'll need the following parts to build your project:

- Coroplast: I found mine on Amazon. It's readily available and can be found in a variety of sizes.

- Plywood: The bottom of the cube will be plywood: anything reasonably heavy will work.

- Box cutter

- Black spray paint

- Wood strips: Any scrap wood will do that's around 1″ by 1″ across and a foot long.

- Wood glue

- Wood screws, #10 × 0.5″

- Arduino UNO: The classic Arduino is sold by SparkFun (P/N 11021) and Adafruit (P/N 50), among countless others.

- NeoPixel Jewel: Available from Adafruit, P/N 2226.

- 9V power supply: Adafruit P/N 63.

Assemble the Pumpkin

The pumpkin cube can be easily put together. Just follow these steps:

1. Cut the Coroplast Sheets to Size

Use your box cutter to cut five Coroplast sheets into 12″×12″ squares, as shown in Figure 7-3. The stuff cuts like butter, all except the support ridges. You might have to make a few cuts to make sure you got all the way through.

2. Cut Out the Face

Apply the face stencil found in the downloads (https://github.com/n1/ MinecraftMakers); then use your box cutter to cut out the eyes and face. The plastic might cut a little tight, but that's all right. The game element looks very rough and creepy, so you don't want neat anyway (Figure 7-4).

FIGURE 7-3: Cut the Coroplast sheets to size.

FIGURE 7-4: Apply the stencil and then cut out the eyes and mouth.

3. Paint the Face

Now is a good time to paint the black parts of the face. Cut away the edge of the eyes and mouth, shown as gray in the pattern; then spray-paint the face black. Figure 7-5 shows the freshly painted face.

Glue parchment behind the holes as you did with the Redstone Lamp project in Chapter 4. Figure 7-5 shows the face with the eyes and mouth cut out.

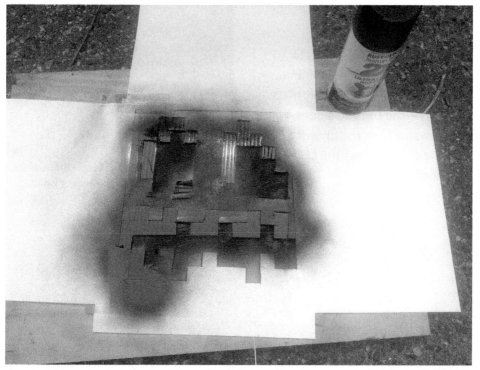

FIGURE 7-5: Use parchment to diffuse the LEDs' light.

4. Glue the Support Frame

The Coroplast panels will be attached to a light wooden frame that I glued together (Figure 7-6) out of scrap wood. Make it 12″ by 12″ and about half an inch thick.

5. Attach the Top Panel to the Support Frame

Use #10 × 0.5″ wood screws to attach the top panel to the frame, as shown in Figure 7-7. The Coroplast assembly—the top and sides—will be removable from the plywood base, allowing you to adjust the LED light as needed.

FIGURE 7-6: Glue together a frame of wood.

FIGURE 7-7: Add the frame of wood strips around the top.

6. Attach the Sides

The top's support frame allows you to attach the Coroplast to the sides. Finish the Coroplast shade (Figure 7-8) by adding the remaining panels, securing them to the top frame with #10 × 0.5″ wood screws and taping the sides. Feel free to add more pieces of wood at the joints if the shade seems shaky.

You're ready to add the electronics, which brings us to the next section!

7. Build the Bottom

The bottom consists of a heavy plywood base. Glue blocks in the corners (as Figure 7-9 shows) to keep the shade from falling off. This works very similar to how the Redstone Lamp worked in

FIGURE 7-8: **Add one side of the pumpkin.**

Chapter 5, with the shade sitting on a base and held in place by a few pieces of wood. When the glue dries, paint the entire base brown or orange.

FIGURE 7-9: **Position pieces of wood to help keep the shade in place.**

Creating a Flickering Flame

The flame effect of the Jack O'Lantern is accomplished by using LEDs and modulating them to simulate the way a real flame looks. Of course, you could just buy an artificial candle from the department store, but we're aiming a little higher than that. Here are three DIY resources for making flame effects:

- Evil Mad Scientist Flickery Flame: The Flickery Flame Kit (evilmadscientist.com, P/N 792), created by legendary Halloween pranksters EMS, is literally designed to be put into pumpkins to light them up. A half-dozen LEDs give a warm glow (Figure 7-10), and the flickering is controlled by a pre-programmed microchip. Just solder it together and power up!

FIGURE 7-10: The Flickery Flame Kit uses a variety of LEDs to give off a natural flicker.

- Flickering LEDs: If the Flickery Flame Kit is too basic, you can also buy the individual flickering LEDs from EMS, including a nice assortment, P/N 748, seen in Figure 7-11. Each LED has a tiny chip embedded in the plastic that gives the light an authentic flicker. Combining reds and yellows gives you a more natural flame effect.

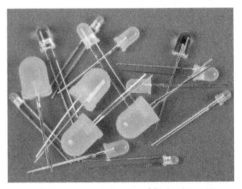

FIGURE 7-11: An assortment of flickering LEDs

- Adafruit NeoPixel Jewel: Let's level up big time. NeoPixels are RGB LEDs with individual chips, allowing them to be daisy-chained almost indefinitely. The product pictured in Figure 7-12 is a Jewel connected to an Arduino clone. The Jewel we'll use (adafruit.com, P/N 2226) has seven LEDs, but Adafruit sells many configurations. NeoPixels are shockingly cheap, with the Jewel ringing up at less than $6. This is the product I used to make my flickering flame, mostly because I had one on hand, but also because it's very bright and readily controllable.

Wiring Up the NeoPixel Jewel

Because the Jewel has seven backlit RGB LEDs, you can create some rather dramatic animations when combined with an Arduino. To assemble the project, you'll need to solder wires to the Jewel. Once the project is assembled, you'll program the Arduino with the code needed to make the Jewel flicker like a flame. Whoa! Does this sound like a lot? Never fear, the Appendix explains all about Arduino and how to upload code.

FIGURE 7-12: **The NeoPixel Jewel features seven bright LEDs.**

8. Solder the Power Wire

Solder a short (1.5″–2″) wire to the pin marked 5V, as shown in Figure 7-13. Leave about ¼″ or ⅓″ of wire bare at the end so it can be attached to the Arduino.

9. Solder the Ground Wire

Solder another wire to one of the ground pins of the Jewel, as shown in Figure 7-14. There are two, and you can use either one. Use a short wire as you did with the 5V wire.

FIGURE 7-13: **Solder a wire to the 5V pin.**

FIGURE 7-14: **Attach a wire to one of the Ground pins.**

10. Solder the Data Wire

Next, solder a third wire to the Data Input pin, as shown in Figure 7-15.

11. Attach the Jewel to the Arduino

The three wires soldered to the Jewel can be inserted into the female headers on the Arduino, with nothing but friction keeping them in place. Figure 7-16 shows a wiring diagram illustrating how each wire connects: 5V on the Jewel connects to 5V on the Arduino, GND to GND, and Data to digital pin 6.

Finally, you have to program the Arduino and power it up to see the effect.

FIGURE 7-15: **Solder a wire to the Data Input pin.**

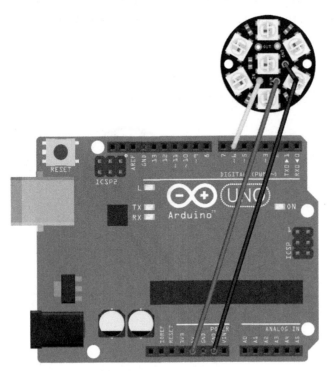

FIGURE 7-16: **Wire up the Arduino.**

Programming the Flame

I used the following code to program a flame-like effect for my NeoPixel Jewel. You can find the code along with the other downloads at github.com/n1/ MinecraftMakers.

```
#include <Adafruit_NeoPixel.h>
#define PIN 6
// Parameter 1 = number of pixels in strip
// Parameter 2 = pin number (most are valid)
// Parameter 3 = pixel type flags, add together as needed:
//   NEO_KHZ800  800 KHz bitstream (most NeoPixel products w/WS2812 LEDs)
//   NEO_KHZ400  400 KHz (classic 'v1' (not v2) FLORA pixels, WS2811 drivers)
//   NEO_GRB     Pixels are wired for GRB bitstream (most NeoPixel products)
//   NEO_RGB     Pixels are wired for RGB bitstream (v1 FLORA pixels, not v2)
Adafruit_NeoPixel strip = Adafruit_NeoPixel(7, PIN, NEO_GRB + NEO_KHZ800);
void setup() {
  strip.begin();
  strip.show(); // Initialize all pixels to 'off'
}
void loop() {
  strip.setPixelColor(0, 160, 40, 0);
  strip.setPixelColor(1, 160, 160, 0);
  strip.setPixelColor(2, 160, 40, 0);
  strip.setPixelColor(3, 0, 0, 0);
  strip.setPixelColor(4, 160, 40, 0);
  strip.setPixelColor(5, 160, 40, 0);
  strip.setPixelColor(6, 160, 40, 0);
  strip.show();
  delay(50);
  strip.setPixelColor(0, 80, 20, 0);
  strip.setPixelColor(1, 0, 0, 0);
  strip.setPixelColor(2, 160, 40, 0);
  strip.setPixelColor(3, 80, 20, 0);
  strip.setPixelColor(4, 100, 60, 0);
  strip.setPixelColor(5, 80, 20, 0);
  strip.setPixelColor(6, 160, 160, 0);
  strip.show();
  delay(50);
    strip.setPixelColor(0, 255, 40, 0);
  strip.setPixelColor(1, 80, 0, 0);
  strip.setPixelColor(2, 160, 20, 0);
```

```
  strip.setPixelColor(3, 0, 0, 0);
  strip.setPixelColor(4, 160, 160, 0);
  strip.setPixelColor(5, 100, 60, 0);
  strip.setPixelColor(6, 160, 40, 0);
  strip.show();
  delay(50);
    strip.setPixelColor(0, 160, 20, 0);
  strip.setPixelColor(1, 255, 40, 0);
  strip.setPixelColor(2, 160, 80, 0);
  strip.setPixelColor(3, 80, 10, 0);
  strip.setPixelColor(4, 0, 0, 0);
  strip.setPixelColor(5, 160, 20, 0);
  strip.setPixelColor(6, 0, 0, 0);
  strip.show();
  delay(50);
}
```

SUMMARY

This project introduced you the intriguing world of Arduino, preparing you for the next two projects. You also ended up with a Minecraft Jack O'Lantern, the perfect decoration for your front steps, as you can see in Figure 7-17.

FIGURE 7-17: The Jack O'Lantern awaits the next trick-or-treater.

Night and Day Clock

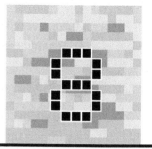

Everyone has a clock on their wall, but not everyone has a Minecraft clock. This game element resembles a disc decorated with night and day imagery on it, which rotates along with the game's cycle, so if you're in a cave and want to know the time, you need only look at your clock.

Your real-life version (seen in Figure 8-1) will also rotate with the minutes and hours, though you may find the display rather cryptic because there are no minute and hour hands. Instead, the disc rotates and you'll have to guess the minutes by gauging the position of the disc. If you need extra help, you can always draw little lines on the disc. Let's get started!

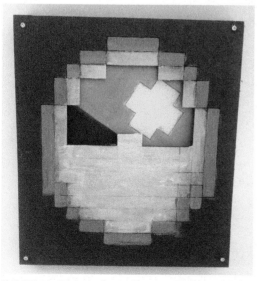

FIGURE 8-1: Curious about the time? Just glance at your Night and Day Clock.

TELLING TIME

It turns out telling time both in the game and outside of it presents challenges. Let's examine both in Minecraft and in the real world.

In Minecraft

As you probably know if you play Minecraft in Survival mode, night and day are very important in the game. In the night, Skeletons and Zombies come out to play, and Spiders turn aggressive. The game has the following times set:

Daytime: 10 minutes

Sunset: 1.5 minutes

Nighttime: 7 minutes

Sunrise: 1.5 minutes

As I mentioned, the best way to tell time in the game are clocks, which are handheld items unless placed in an Item Frame, as shown in Figure 8-2. Just the ticket for ensuring your Steve doesn't walk out of a cave and get jumped by hostile mobs.

FIGURE 8-2: The clock tells when it's safe to come out of your cave.

Needless to say, making a real-world version of the clock (complete with Item Frame) doesn't make sense if you use Minecraft's 20-minute cycle. What we want is a clock that tells us real-world time.

In the Real World

Telling time with an Arduino works well for short periods of time and then stops working. What happens is that the Arduino uses memory to keep track of the time, but after a while its memory fills up and the clock won't keep up.

The solution lies in a special chip called an RTC (Real-Time Clock). This chip is mounted on a small circuit board (Figure 8-3) with a timing crystal and a battery backup so it will remember the time even if the main project loses power.

However, just because the RTC-equipped 'Duino *knows* the time doesn't mean it has the means to display it. The project you'll build uses a motor to turn the disc once every 24 hours, and markings on the disc will thereby display the time.

FIGURE 8-3: The RTC module you'll use in this project

Building the Minecraft Clock

Our real-life version of the Minecraft clock consists of a plywood panel for the disc and another for the outside part, which I'm calling the case. On the back of the clock, a motor, Arduino, and RTC module take care of business.

Design It

As you've done a bunch already, it's time to count pixels. Looking at the clock in the game, it's evident that there is a disc with both night and day scenes on it. The disc rotates behind the case so you can only see the relevant time of day. Figure 8-4 shows a diagram of the disc: it's a circle divided in two, with a sun on one side and a moon on the other. In addition, you can see the mounting holes for attaching the disc to the motor.

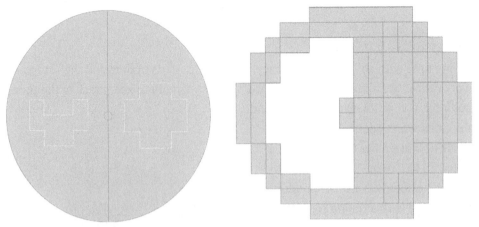

FIGURE 8-4: Use this pattern to cut and decorate your clock pieces.

We also need to build the case. In the game, the case is the same size as the disc. However, in the real world we'll need it a little bit bigger so that it can be attached to the background board. The design shown in Figure 8-5 shows the case, complete with mounting holes.

Parts and Tools

You'll need some familiar parts and tools to build the disc and case, but most of the electronics is all new. Here's what you'll need:

▦ Plywood: I'm suggesting ⅛″ thickness to save on weight.

▦ Arduino UNO

▦ RTC: I used the DS1307 breakout from Adafruit.

▦ Adafruit Motor Shield, P/N 1438

▦ Power supply: 9V wall wart such as Adafruit P/N 63

FIGURE 8-5: The case will be mounted to partly cover the disc.

- Stepper motor: I used Adafruit's 5V Small Reduction Stepper Motor, P/N 858.

- Limit switch: The one I used is pictured in Figure 8-6. You can buy a similar one from Servo City, P/N 605634.

- Shaft coupler, 6mm to ¼": SparkFun P/N 12211

- D-shaft: I used a ¼"×1.25" axle from Servo City, P/N 634060. You can use any ¼" rod, including what you could find in your local hardware store.

- Clamping hub, 1.4" SparkFun P/N 12238

- #4 hardware: There are a million places on the Internet to get #4 screws in a variety of lengths, and nuts and washers as well.

- #6 screws; you can buy these from SparkFun.

FIGURE 8-6: **This switch will tell the Arduino when to set midnight.**

- Aluminum standoffs: SparkFun has these as well.

Tools

You'll also need the usual woodshop tools you've used throughout the book:

- Band saw

- Drill and a variety of bits

Build the Enclosure

Let's start by building the case and disc.

1. Apply the Templates and Cut

You know the drill—or saw, I suppose. Glue the templates (found in https:// github.com/n1/MinecraftMakers) onto some plywood, as seen in Figure 8-7.

FIGURE 8-7: **Cut out the templates.**

I'm suggesting eighth-inch but feel free to use whatever works for you. Sand the pieces when they're cut.

2. Paint the Enclosure

Paint the pieces of the enclosure because it's easier to do it now than when the electronics are installed. Figure 8-8 shows me touching up the paint on my clock.

Wire Up the Electronics

Now for the challenging part. You'll attach the various components together and to the back of the clock.

3. Attach the Arduino

Use #4 hardware to attach the Arduino to the back, as shown in Figure 8-9. Once you're ready to test out the project, you can power the Arduino with the 9V wall wart specified in the parts list.

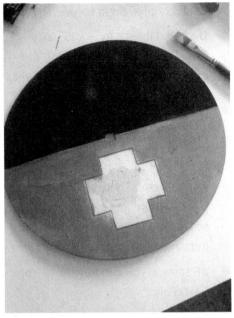

FIGURE 8-8: Paint the case and disc before assembly.

FIGURE 8-9: Use #4 screws to attach the Arduino to the back.

4. Install the Motor Shield

The motor shield (Figure 8-10) sits right on top of the Arduino, with the shield's male headers connecting with the Arduino's female headers.

5. Attach the RTC

The RTC module (Figure 8-11) comes with mounting holes. Use #4 hardware to attach the module to the back, with wires soldered as you see in Figure 8-10: GND and 5V go to the appropriate pins on the Arduino, and SDA (the yellow wire) and SCL (the green wire) to analog pins 4 and 5, respectively.

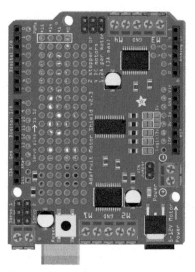

FIGURE 8-10: **Attach the motor shield.**

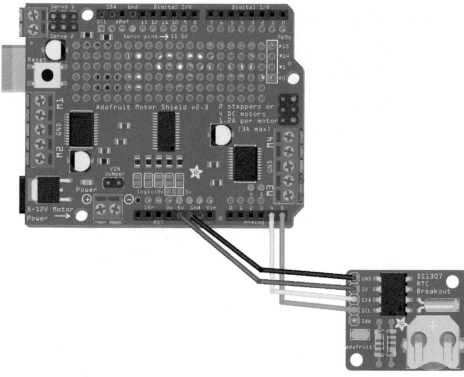

FIGURE 8-11: **Attach the RTC.**

6. Install the Stepper Motor

Use #4 hardware to attach the motor so that the axle projects through the black board. Figure 8-12 shows how it should look. Wiring it up is a cinch: the red and orange wires connect to the motor ports marked M4 and the pink and blue wires connect to M3, with the central yellow wire going to GND. Figure 8-13 shows how easily the stepper is wired in.

FIGURE 8-12: **Install the stepper motor.**

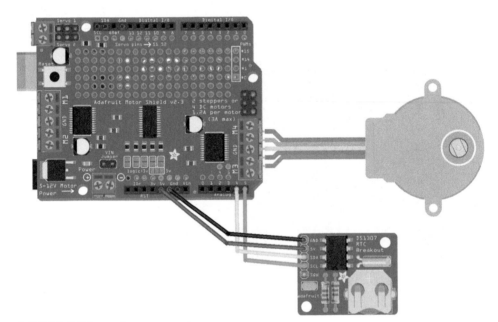

FIGURE 8-13: **Wire up the stepper motor.**

7. Attach the Limit Switch

Position the limit switch (Figure 8-14) so that the disc trips it at midnight. I glued a small block of wood to the disc, waiting until I had found the perfect position for the limit switch. If you don't want to use a limit switch, you'd have to restart the program with the disc set for midnight every time, as the stepper motor has no idea what position it's at.

Connect one lead of the switch to 5V (the purple wire in Figure 8-15) and the other to Digital Pin 2, also connecting to GND via a 10K resistor.

FIGURE 8-14: **Install the limit switch.**

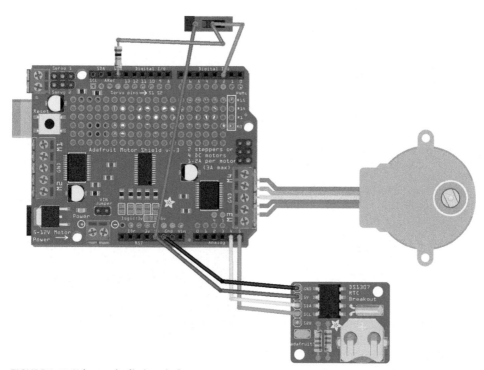

FIGURE 8-15: **Wire up the limit switch.**

8. Attach the Stepper Hardware

The shaft adapter, axle, and clamping hub (seen connected in Figure 8-16) can be attached to the stepper's shaft. The clamping hub is on the axle just for a spacing purpose at the moment, because in the next step you'll be attaching it to the disc.

Finish the Project

Now to finish the project by putting it together!

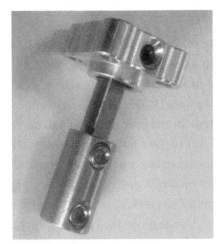

FIGURE 8-16: **Attach the stepper hardware.**

9. Attach the Disc

Temporarily remove the clamping hub from the axle and attach it to the disc using its four mounting holes, as shown in Figure 8-17. The hub uses #6 screws, and you'll have to drill holes in the disc to accommodate them. Secure the hub to the axle again when you're done.

10. Attach the Face

Use #6 standoffs and hardware (Figure 8-18) to attach the face to the back piece of plywood.

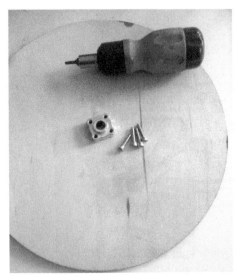

FIGURE 8-17: **Attach the disc.**

FIGURE 8-18: **Use standoffs to attach the face.**

Program the Clock

Upload the following code to your Arduino:

```
#include <Wire.h>
#include "RTClib.h"
#include <Adafruit_MotorShield.h>
#include "utility/Adafruit_PWMServoDriver.h"
RTC_DS1307 RTC;
Adafruit_MotorShield AFMS = Adafruit_MotorShield();
Adafruit_StepperMotor *myMotor = AFMS.getStepper(513, 2);
const int limitSwitch = 3;
void setup() {
  Serial.begin(9600);
  Wire.begin();
  RTC.begin();
  AFMS.begin();
  if (! RTC.isrunning()) {
    Serial.println("RTC is NOT running!");
    // following line sets the RTC to the date & time this sketch was
compiled
    RTC.adjust(DateTime(__DATE__, __TIME__));
  }
  myMotor->setSpeed(10);  // 10 rpm
```

This next step is cool: it calls a function that calibrates the disc so that it points to the right angle. The truth is that the stepper motor has no idea on which step it currently sits.

```
  calibrate_Stepper();
}
void loop() {
  int currentStep;
//let's determine the time according to the RTC.
  DateTime now = RTC.now();
  int hourDisplay = (now.hour(), DEC);
  Serial.print(hourDisplay);
  Serial.print(':');
```

```
int minuteDisplay = (now.minute(), DEC);

Serial.println(minuteDisplay);

//total time elapsed since midnight

int minutesElapsed=((hourDisplay * 60) + minuteDisplay);

//map minutesElapsed: 24:00 (minute 1440) maps to 513 to get number

//of steps

int timeSteps = map(minutesElapsed, 0, 1440, 0, 513);


  Serial.print("minutes elapsed: ");

 Serial.print(minutesElapsed);

   Serial.print("equals this number of steps: ");

      Serial.println(timeSteps);

//while statement telling the Arduino how many steps to take

while (currentStep < timeSteps) {

  myMotor->step(1, FORWARD, MICROSTEP);

 }

}
```

Here is the function I mentioned. On startup, the Arduino rotates the disk one step at a time, listening to the limit switch. When the switch is tripped, it sets currentStep to 0.

```
void calibrate_Stepper() {

  while (digitalRead(limitSwitch) == LOW)

  {

    myMotor->step(1, FORWARD, MICROSTEP);

  }

  int currentStep = 0;

  delay(10);

}
```

SUMMARY

In this, the penultimate project in the book, you got a chance to try out some more complicated Arduino techniques. Hopefully your Night and Day Clock finds a home on your wall or on a shelf (Figure 8-19). It may not be the most easily read clock in the world, but you made it yourself!

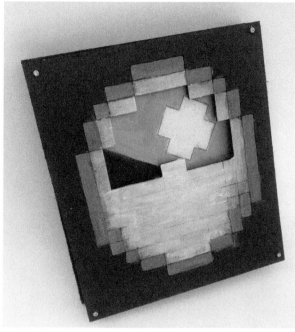

FIGURE 8-19: **The Night and Day Clock, completed**

Robot Creeper

You knew there had to be a monster Creeper project in the book and here it is. You're going to build a motorized Creeper (Figure 9-1) with a metal skeleton and wooden skin. Aside from the fact that the thing most certainly doesn't blow up, you'll love it, and you'll learn a lot about robotics and Arduino along the way. Let's get to it!

FIGURE 9-1: **Build this Creeper.**

BUILDING THE ROBOT CREEPER

The Creeper consists of a robot chassis kit with add-on parts creating the mob's distinctive armless body, with a motor in back of the neck to turn the head around. Begin by taking a look at the Creeper in-game. Just be sure to stick to Creative mode or you may find yourself getting blown up!

The Creeper in Minecraft

As you can easily see in Figure 9-2, the Creeper consists of a cubical head 8 pixels on a side, a 4×8×12 body, and four 4×8×4 legs. It's actually a pretty elegant design, which makes it a breeze for building a physical re-creation.

FIGURE 9-2: **The Creeper sports a surprisingly simple design.**

Build the Robot Creeper

Let's face it: a full-scale Creeper would be a monster, literally—over 4 feet high. Let's see what we can do to bring that down a little. The next thing to do is figure out a scale that works with the robotics parts, particularly the chassis kit we're using for the base.

Design It

The Robot Creeper seems super challenging at first. The thing has to *look* like a Creeper, ideally proportionate with the game element. At the same time, it also has to *function* as a robot. In other words, regardless of its outer appearance, the Creeper has to be able to fit all the necessary robotic components.

I began with a robot kit called the Actobotics Bogie Runt Rover, a kit available for around $70 that comes with a chassis, six motors, and six wheels. The assembled rover's chassis measures 6″×9″, though the wheels project a little from that. On the other hand, it rides fairly high: 6 inches off the ground. With that measurement in my head, I was able to decide on the size of the footprint: 12″×8″, or—conveniently—one inch per pixel.

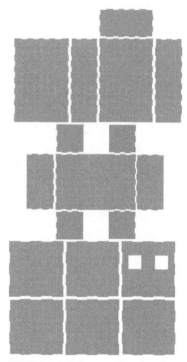

Applying the one-inch scale across the whole robot makes for a 12″-high, 8″-wide, and 4″-deep body, an 8″ cubical head, as well as four legs 6×4×4. However, for the legs I decided to merge the front pair and back pair into 8″-wide blocks—the thing is going to roll, not walk. Figure 9-3 shows my final design.

Next up, we need to design the robot's electronics. What will be its functionality? How will it be controlled? The Minecraft Creeper is known for blowing up, and clearly that was out. It also turns its head, and we can do that by putting a servo motor inside the body that turns the robot's head. The Creeper also has eyes that turn red when it's about to explode. That's easy! We'll put a NeoPixel Jewel in the head just like we did with the Jack O'Lantern.

FIGURE 9-3: **A diagram showing the design**

About Actobotics

Add-on parts abound for the Bogie Runt Rover kit. I'm talking about structural elements and a plethora of well-made robot parts that are called Actobotics. They offer everything from axles and bearings to connector plates and motor mounts. Best of all, the entire line is completely compatible with one another. That means we can take an Actobotics rover and easily add Actobotics parts to create a new robot.

Actobotics' signature component are their channels, an assortment of which can be seen in this figure. They come in a multitude of lengths and are liberally peppered with connector holes, allowing them to be used as the backbone of any number of projects.

You can learn more about the product line at their home site, servocity.com. SparkFun.com has a wide assortment of Actobotics parts as well. These sites sell individual parts as well as kits and assortments, and from here you should be able to buy the parts needed for the project.

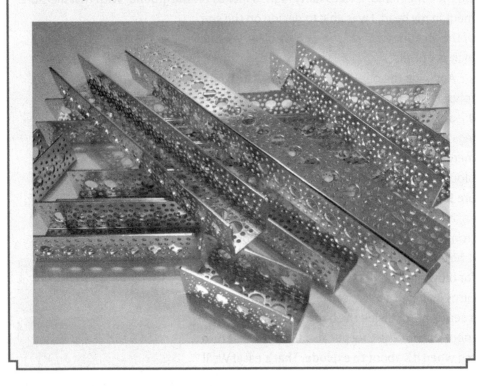

Under the hood I stuck with the classic Arduino Uno, with a motor control shield sitting on top. This add-on board helps the Arduino manage the high voltages needed to run motors, and it simplifies controlling them.

Speaking of control, I'm making a simplified controller (Figure 9-4) that connects to the robot via a trio of wires.

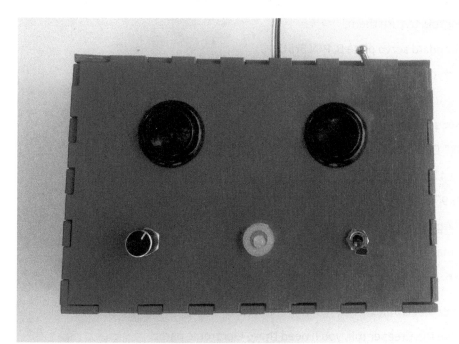

FIGURE 9-4: **Steer your robot with this handheld controller.**

Parts and Tools

You'll need a lot of parts for this one, ranging from wood to mechanical parts and electronics.

Wood and Hardware

Unsurprisingly, you'll need to put in some work at the woodshop. Here's what you'll need:

▪ ¼″ and ⅛″ plywood—the same stuff you've been using throughout this book

▪ Wood glue

Actobotics Parts

You also need a variety of robotics parts:

- Actobotics Bogie Runt Rover Kit —Servocity.com P/N 637162. This kit is $70 on its own. However, you get a high-quality rover for your money. The kit comes with an indestructible ABS plate for top, six knobby off-road wheels, and six motors to turn them.
- Standard servo plate B, P/N 575124
- Servo to 0.25″ coupler, P/N HSA250
- ¼″ quad pillow block, P/N 535130
- Set screw hub, P/N 545548
- 12″ D-shaft, P/N 634094
- 2×4″ channels
- 1×9″ channel
- Large square screw plate, P/N 585430
- Small square screw plate, P/N 585478
- #6-32 socket-head screws in a variety of lengths

Creeper Electronics

To make the Creeper roll, you'll need these electronic parts:

- Arduino UNO
- Adafruit motor shield, Adafruit P/N 1438
- NeoPixel Jewel, P/N 2226
- Servo: A no-name servo such as Adafruit P/N 1142 does the trick.
- Wire: I'm a fan of SparkFun's wire assortment, P/N 11367.
- Servo extension wire, Adafruit P/N 973

Controller Electronics

And to make the handheld controller:

- Arduino UNO
- 2 arcade buttons: I used standard buttons, similar to Adafruit P/N 473 except mine are opaque black.

- 2 switches: Standard single-pole, single-throw (SPST) toggle switches such as SparkFun P/N 9276

- Potentiometer: SparkFun P/N 9939 works.

- RGB LED: You'll be using only two colors of this LED, SparkFun P/N 105.

- Long, three-strand wire. SparkFun sells a 15´, 10-wire strand (P/N 10647) that could be torn down to three-wire.

Build the Chassis

Begin the build by tackling the robot's metal and plastic skeleton, starting with the rover kit.

1. Assemble the Rover Kit

I won't provide step-by-steps for the Bogie Runt Rover, seen in Figure 9-5. Servo City provides a great assembly video on YouTube: just search for it.

FIGURE 9-5: The Bogie Runt Rover is your starting point.

2. Add the Body Base

Attach one of the 3.5″ pieces of channel to the center set of mounting holes on the rover, using a large square screw plate and four screws added from the underside. Figure 9-6 shows the channel secured to the chassis.

3. Attach the Head Servo

Use the standard servo plate to attach the servo to the channel. While you're at it, you can attach the coupler that attaches the motor's shaft to the D-rod. Figure 9-7 shows how it should look.

FIGURE 9-6: **Add a 3.5″ piece of channel.**

FIGURE 9-7: Attach the servo to the channel.

4. Attach the Body Channel

Secure a 9″ piece of channel to the 3.5″ piece you already attached. Use a double screw plate as shown in Figure 9-8.

5. Add the Support Beam

Attach the second 3.5″ channel (Figure 9-9) at the top of the 9″ piece using a double screw plate.

6. Attach the Bearing

Attach the bearing so that it lines up with the servo's shaft. Figure 9-10 shows how it should look.

FIGURE 9-8: Attach the 9″ channel.

FIGURE 9-9: Add a second 3.5″ channel.

FIGURE 9-10: Attach the bearing.

7. Secure the D-Rod

Thread the D-rod through the bearing and secure it in the servo's coupler, as shown in Figure 9-11.

Adding the Skin

The Creeper's skin consists of a series of wooden box shapes that rely on gravity to stay on the robot. You will find the construction methods you perfected throughout the projects in this book perfect for the Creeper's skin.

8. Assemble the Feet and Body Portions

FIGURE 9-11: Secure the D-rod in the servo's coupler.

As mentioned, the feet and body are merely a series of boxes, as seen in Figure 9-12. You've been making boxes throughout this book. You can find the blueprint for the feet and body among the downloads for this book, https://github.com/n1/MinecraftMakers.

FIGURE 9-12: Assemble the body.

9. Paint It!

It's time to paint the body and feet that delightful Creeper green. Figure 9-13 shows my creation with one coat of paint.

10. Attach the Skin

Once the paint is dry, drop it down on the robot (Figure 9-14) with the ¼″ rod projecting from the top. It should fit nicely without any problem.

11. Add the Head Base

The head will remind you a lot of the Redstone Lamp project in that it has a heavier base, with a lighter "shade" resting on top. Let's use quarter-inch plywood, 8″ by 8″. Drill a 0.25″ center hole as well as the mounting holes for the hub; then secure the hub with the small square screw plate. Figure 9-15 shows the base.

FIGURE 9-13: **Paint the body.**

FIGURE 9-14: **Attach the skin.**

FIGURE 9-15: **Attach the head base.**

12. Build the Head

Assemble the panels of the head (Figure 9-16). Once again, a plywood box! This one needs holes for eyes.

13. Paint the Head

Paint the outside of the head green to match the skin, but also add the black parts of the face. Also, I suggest painting the *inside* of the head black (Figure 9-17) so the eyes look blacker.

FIGURE 9-16: **Build the head!**

FIGURE 9-17: **Paint the head.**

Add the Electronics

Now for my favorite part: adding the Arduino, motor shield, battery pack, and so forth.

14. Install the Arduino

Find a spot on the underneath of the robot to install the Arduino using #4 hardware (Figure 9-18). You can drill into the Bogie's ABS chassis if you want, or use one of the available mounting holes.

FIGURE 9-18: Just add Arduino!

15. Seat the Motor Shield on the Arduino

You know the drill from the Night and Day Clock project from the previous chapter. Seat the motor shield (Figure 9-19) on top of the Arduino with the pins connected.

16. Connect the Servo

Attach the servo wires to the motor shield's pins, as shown in Figure 9-20.

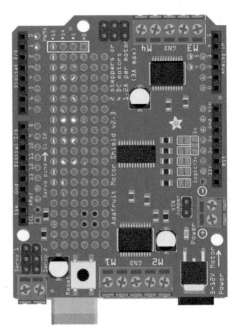

FIGURE 9-19: **Attach the motor shield.**

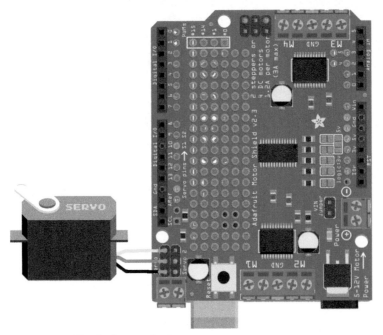

FIGURE 9-20: **Plug in the servo's wires.**

17. Attach the 9V Battery

Attach the 9V battery to the chassis but don't plug it in yet. Figure 9-21 shows it in place. This powers the Arduino but not the motors.

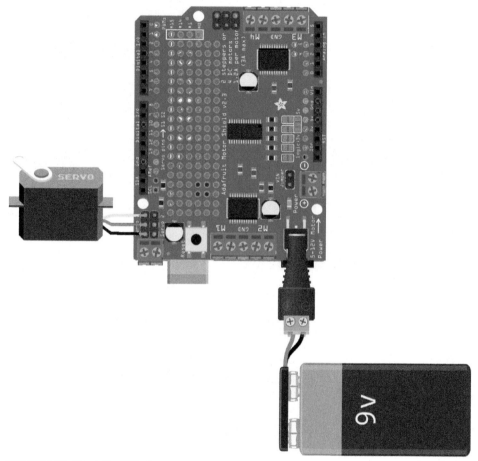

FIGURE 9-21: **Attach the 9V battery.**

18. Attach the Battery Pack

Attach the battery pack to the chassis and plug it into the motor shield, as shown in Figure 9-22. This pack powers the motors separately.

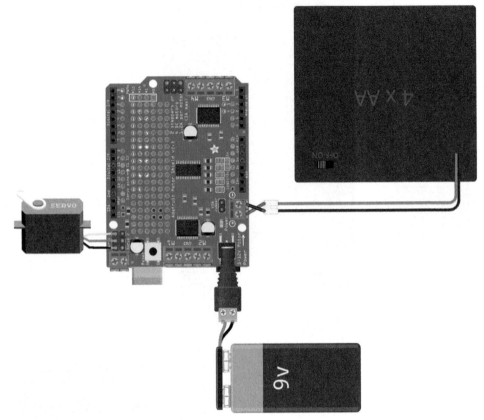

FIGURE 9-22: **Attach the battery pack.**

19. Connect the Motors

You have six motors, three on the left and three on the right. Combine the leads as you see in Figure 9-23, so that M3 controls one side and M4 controls the other. The Bogie's motors are modest in side and stacking them won't strain the motor shield's capabilities.

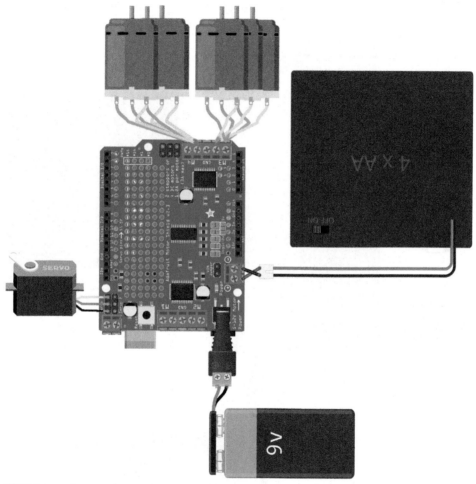

FIGURE 9-23: **Connect the motors.**

20. Wire Up the NeoPixel Eyes

You're using two NeoPixel Jewels for eyes, to create the telltale glowing red that signals an imminent explosion. Connect both the VIN (red wire) and GND (black) pins to the Arduino as shown in Figure 9-24. The data wire goes from Digital Pin 6 on the Arduino to the IN pin on the first Jewel, and then from OUT to IN on the next eye.

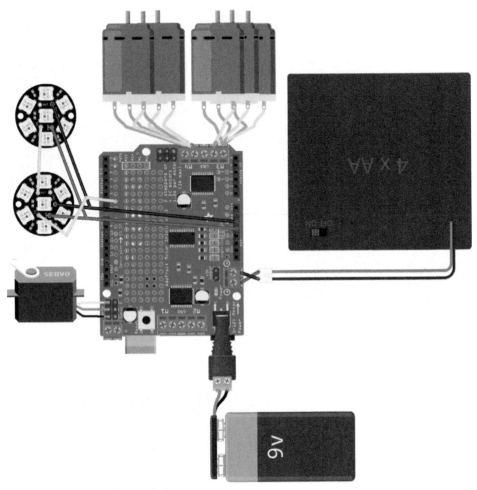

FIGURE 9-24: **Wire up the NeoPixel eyes.**

21. Connect to the Controller

You'll need three wires to attach the Creeper to its controller. As you can see in Figure 9-25, one wire connects to Digital Pin 0 on the Arduino, another one to Pin 1, and a third to GND. They will attach to their counterparts on the controller's Arduino. You can make these wires as long as you want, but 6´ is probably good enough.

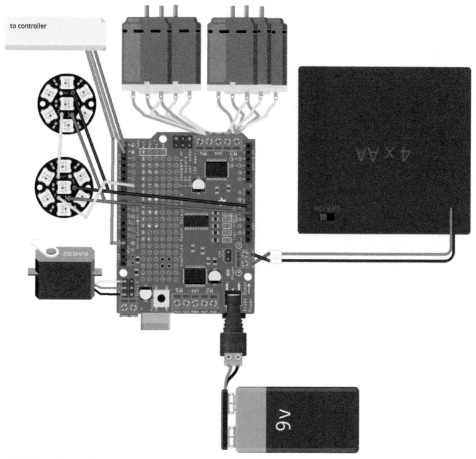

to controller

FIGURE 9-25: **Attach the controller.**

Programming the Creeper

The Creeper is a simple robot, and this is reflected in the code:

```
#include <Wire.h>
#include <Adafruit_MotorShield.h>
#include "utility/Adafruit_PWMServoDriver.h"
#include <Servo.h>
#include <Adafruit_NeoPixel.h>
Adafruit_MotorShield AFMS = Adafruit_MotorShield();
Adafruit_DCMotor *leftMotors = AFMS.getMotor(3);
Adafruit_DCMotor *rightMotors = AFMS.getMotor(4);
Servo servo1;
#define PIN 6
Adafruit_NeoPixel strip = Adafruit_NeoPixel(14, PIN, NEO_GRB + NEO_KHZ800);
const int buzzerPin = 13;
void setup()
{
  Serial.begin(9600);
  AFMS.begin();
  servo1.attach(10);
  strip.begin();
  strip.show(); // Initialize all pixels to 'off'
}
void loop() {
  if (Serial.available() >= 2)
  {
    char start = Serial.read();
    if (start != '*')
    {
      return;
    }
    char cmd = Serial.read();
    process_incoming_command(cmd);
  }
  delay(50); //limit how fast we update
}
void process_incoming_command(char cmd)
{
  int speed = 0;
```

```
switch (cmd)
{
case 0:
  //DO NOTHING
  break;
case 1:
  //DRIVE LEFT WHEELS
  leftMotors->setSpeed(200);
  leftMotors->run(RELEASE);
  break;
case 2:
  //DRIVE RIGHT WHEELS
  rightMotors->setSpeed(200);
  rightMotors->run(RELEASE);
  break;
case 3:
  //TURN ON EYES
  strip.setPixelColor(0, 255, 0, 0);
  strip.setPixelColor(1, 255, 0, 0);
  strip.setPixelColor(2, 255, 0, 0);
  strip.setPixelColor(3, 255, 0, 0);
  strip.setPixelColor(4, 255, 0, 0);
  strip.setPixelColor(5, 255, 0, 0);
  strip.setPixelColor(6, 255, 0, 0);
  strip.setPixelColor(7, 255, 0, 0);
  strip.setPixelColor(8, 255, 0, 0);
  strip.setPixelColor(9, 255, 0, 0);
  strip.setPixelColor(10, 255, 0, 0);
  strip.setPixelColor(11, 255, 0, 0);
  strip.setPixelColor(12, 255, 0, 0);
  strip.setPixelColor(13, 255, 0, 0);
  strip.show();
  break;
case 4:
  //TURN OFF EYES
  strip.setPixelColor(0, 0, 0, 0);
  strip.setPixelColor(1, 0, 0, 0);
  strip.setPixelColor(2, 0, 0, 0);
  strip.setPixelColor(3, 0, 0, 0);
```

```
          strip.setPixelColor(4, 0, 0, 0);
          strip.setPixelColor(5, 0, 0, 0);
          strip.setPixelColor(6, 0, 0, 0);
          strip.setPixelColor(7, 0, 0, 0);
          strip.setPixelColor(8, 0, 0, 0);
          strip.setPixelColor(9, 0, 0, 0);
          strip.setPixelColor(10, 0, 0, 0);
          strip.setPixelColor(11, 0, 0, 0);
          strip.setPixelColor(12, 0, 0, 0);
          strip.setPixelColor(13, 0, 0, 0);
          strip.show();
          break;
        case 5:
          //TURN HEAD 90DEG LEFT
          servo1.write(0);
          delay(15);
          break;
        case 6:
          //TURN HEAD 45DEG LEFT
          servo1.write(45);
          delay(15);
          break;
        case 7:
          //TURN HEAD FORWARD
          servo1.write(90);
          delay(15);
          break;
        case 8:
          //TURN HEAD 45DEG RIGHT
          servo1.write(135);
          delay(15);
          break;
        case 9:
          //TURN HEAD 90DEG RIGHT
          servo1.write(180);
          delay(15);
          break;
      }
    }
```

Building the Controller

The controller I built is a simple plywood box 6″ by 4″ by 2″, and it fits nicely in my hand.

1. Assemble the Box

Go for it! As usual, I'm including the vectors for my controller in with the book's downloads. I painted the box purple just for fun, and it doesn't resemble anything found in the game. Spoiler alert: Figure 9-26 shows the completed controller.

FIGURE 9-26: **Make yet another box.**

2. Install the Arduino

Use wood screws to attach the Arduino to the bottom of the controller box (Figure 9-27).

3. Wire Up the Buttons

Take the breadboard specified in the parts list and attach the two buttons and the switch that turns on the eyes. They all work the same way in Arduino-land. Connect one lead to power (shown as gray wires in Figure 9-28) and the other to the appropriate digital pin on the Arduino. Simultaneously, connect the other lead to GND via a 10K resistor.

FIGURE 9-27: **Attach the Arduino.**

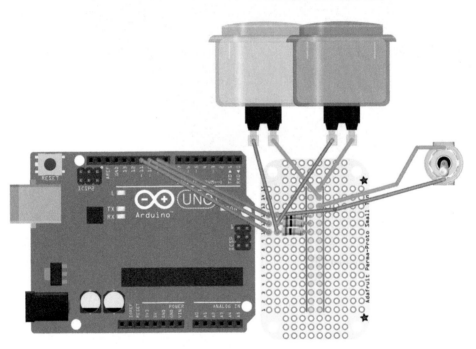

FIGURE 9-28: **Attach the buttons.**

4. Attach the Potentiometer

The first lead connects to power, the third lead connects to GND, and the middle one to pin A0 on the Arduino. Figure 9-29 shows the pot wired up.

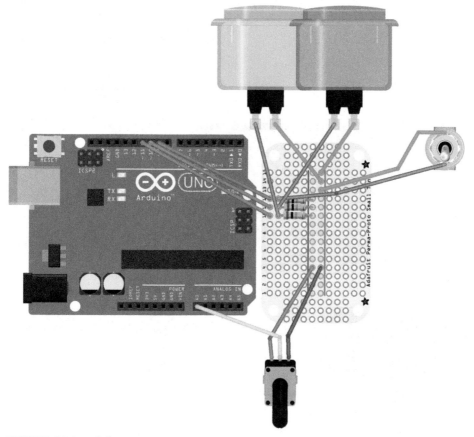

FIGURE 9-29: **Install the pot.**

5. Wire Up the Battery and Power Switch

The other switch controls the power to the Arduino. Wire it in line with the battery pack, as shown in Figure 9-30.

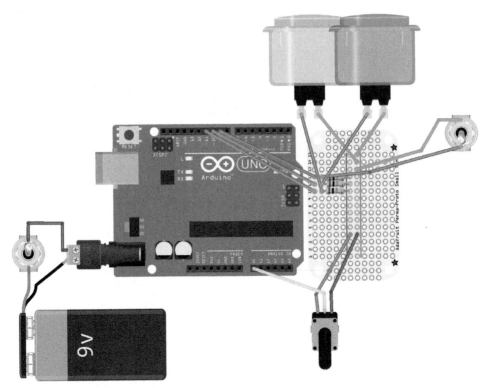

FIGURE 9-30: **Install the battery and power switch.**

6. Install the LED

Connect the LED to the Arduino. Each lead wire gets its own digital pin, while the third goes to GND. If you're using a RGB (tricolor) LED, just ignore the blue lead. Figure 9-31 shows the LED installed.

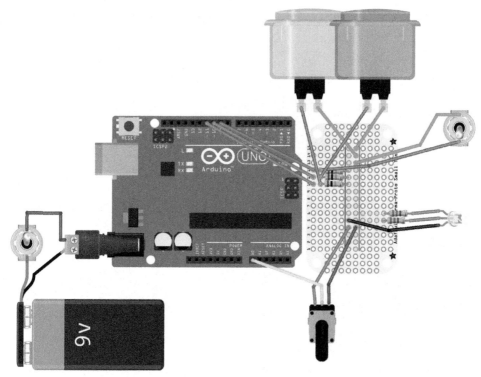

FIGURE 9-31: **Wire up the LED.**

7. Connect to the Robot

Finally, connect to the robot via the three wires (Figure 9-32). Each one connects to the same ports on the Creeper's Arduino. You're ready to roll!

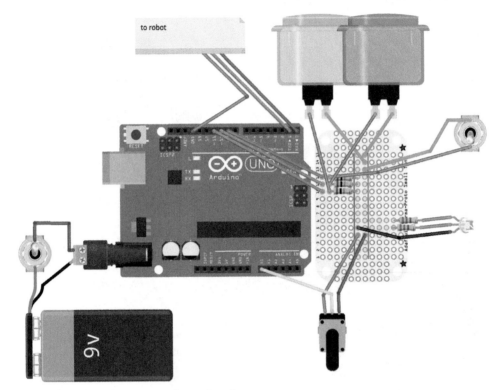

FIGURE 9-32: **Connect the controller to the robot.**

Programming the Controller

Upload the following code to the controller's Arduino:

```
#include <Wire.h>
const int button1Pin = 5;
const int button2Pin = 6;
const int switch1Pin = 9;
const int ledRed = 10;
const int ledGreen = 11;
```

```
const int pot1Pin = A0;
int button1State = 0;
int button2State = 0;
int switch1State = 0;
int pot1State = 0;
void setup()
{
  Serial.begin(9600);
  pinMode(button1Pin, INPUT_PULLUP);
  pinMode(button2Pin, INPUT_PULLUP);
  pinMode(switch1Pin, INPUT_PULLUP);
  pinMode(pot1Pin, INPUT_PULLUP);
  //LED SHINES YELLOW
  digitalWrite(ledRed, HIGH);
  digitalWrite(ledGreen, HIGH);
}
void loop() {
  if (Serial.available() >= 2)
  {
    //LED SHINES GREEN IF SERIAL IS AVAILABLE
    digitalWrite(ledRed, LOW);
    digitalWrite(ledGreen, HIGH);
    //END LEDS
    char start = Serial.read();
    if (start != '*')
    {
      return;
    }
    //LED SHINES RED IF SERIAL IS UNAVAILABLE
    digitalWrite(ledRed, HIGH);
    digitalWrite(ledGreen, LOW);
    //END LEDS
    char cmd = Serial.read();
  }
```

```
button1State = digitalRead(button1Pin);
if (button1State == HIGH) {
  Serial.write('*');
  Serial.write(1);
}
else {
  Serial.write('*');
  Serial.write(0);
}
button2State = digitalRead(button2Pin);
if (button2State == HIGH) {
  Serial.write('*');
  Serial.write(2);
}
else {
  Serial.write('*');
  Serial.write(0);
}
switch1State = digitalRead(switch1Pin);
if (switch1State == HIGH) {
  Serial.write('*');
  Serial.write(3);
}
else {
  Serial.write('*');
  Serial.write(4);
}
//REMAPS POTENTIOMETER VALUE FROM 0-1023 TO 5-9.
pot1State = analogRead(pot1Pin);
int pot1Command = map(pot1State, 0, 5, 1023, 9);
Serial.write('*');
Serial.write(pot1Command);
delay(50); //limit how fast we update
}
```

SUMMARY

And with that, you're done building a rather complicated robot (Figure 9-33)! I hope you enjoyed building this project, and for that matter the other projects in the book. Thanks for reading!

FIGURE 9-33: **The Creeper creeps in the grass.**

Arduino Crash Course

If you've heard of Arduinos but want to learn more, you've come to the right place! Arduinos are microcontrollers, tiny computers that listen to sensors, power lights, and control motors, following a series of programmed instructions. They're dirt easy to use and cost hardly anything by technology standards.

Check out the Arduino UNO in Figure A-1. It's a circuit board about the size of a credit card with mysterious electronic components attached to it. Read on to learn more about this awesome tool.

FIGURE A-1: The UNO serves as the default Arduino.

KNOW YOUR UNO

The UNO isn't the fastest, the newest, or the most powerful Arduino around. However, it's fine for most projects, and there are tons of code examples and tutorials available for it, not to mention add-on sensors and components galore. For these reasons the UNO remains popular, even among tinkerers who have moved on to bigger and better models.

Let's learn a little more about the UNO. Follow along with the callouts in Figure A-2.

1. Reset button—This button restarts the Arduino sketch from the beginning.

2. USB-B socket—This socket accepts a USB-B cord.

3. Barrel plug—Plug a power cord with a 2.1mm barrel into this power socket.

4. Built-in LED—Want to test out the Arduino? The easiest way is to blink this LED. I'll show you how to do this later in this appendix.

5. TX/RX LEDs—These LEDs flash to show that data is flowing. You'll most often see this when uploading to the Arduino.

6. Timing crystal—This 16Hz crystal helps the Arduino keep track of time.

FIGURE A-2: **Learn more about what each component does.**

7. Digital pins—These pins control LEDs, servomotors, and other components.

8. ICSP header—This 6-pin header allows the Arduino's bootloader to be reflashed, or reprogrammed, without removing the board from a hypothetical circuit.

9. ATmega328P—The brains of the Arduino, the 328P is a microcontroller that controls the digital pins and reads data from the analog pins.

10. Power pins—These pins deliver 3.3V or 5V plus ground and a few other bells and whistles.

11. Analog In pins—Finally, there are the Analog In pins, typically used to take readings from sensors.

Put GPIOs to Work

Arduinos interact with the world with the help of their general purpose in/out (GPIO) pins, analog and digital. Digital pins turn on and off to control 5-volt signals, allowing you to power LEDs, trigger motors, and so on. Digital pins can also create dimming effects by turning components on and off very rapidly.

By contrast, analog pins take readings from sensors that deliver a range of possible readings. For instance, a light sensor connected to an analog pin typically delivers a reading from 0 to 1027 depending on the brightness of the detected light.

Figure A-3 is a rendering showing a simple Arduino project. It sounds a buzzer when the button is pressed. The yellow wire in the diagram connects the buzzer to Pin 8 and the orange wire connects the button to Pin 2. The red and black wires provide power and ground.

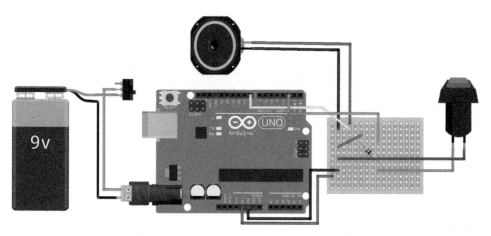

FIGURE A-3: A sample project shows how the pins work.

Powering the UNO

There are three ways to power the Arduino. The first and easiest consists of plugging the board into a computer via a USB cable. This not only powers the Arduino but also serves as a data connection so you can program it. Requiring a computer is one limitation of this method, though a wall-plug adapter or USB-equipped battery can work as well. Figure A-4 shows the Arduino powered up via USB.

There is also a barrel-plug that accommodates battery packs and "wall wart"-style power supplies. A good example of such a power supply is the 9V wall adapter from SparkFun (P/N 298), though you can use a 9V battery with the right plug as well.

Finally, the pin marked Vin near Analog 0 can be used to power the board if you want a soldered connection instead of a plug.

FIGURE A-4: Plug in the UNO and power it up.

Download the Arduino Software

To program the Arduino, you'll need to download the development environment, the Arduino IDE. You can find it at https://www.arduino.cc/ under Software. The environment works on Windows, Linux, and Macintosh computers but the directions differ for each platform, so I suggest you peruse their installation instructions.

SKETCHES: PROGRAMS FOR ARDUINOS

Next up, let's learn how to program the device. Arduino programs are called *sketches*, but they work using the same universal programming techniques that other languages offer, making the process very simple and understandable if you've ever done any programming. Even if you haven't, the syntax is straightforward once you get used to it.

Let's examine Blink, one of the simplest sketches as well as the one newbies typically learn first. Blink does what you expect: it makes an LED blink. More specifically, it makes the built-in LED on the board blink, one second on and one second off.

Go into your Arduino software and select the Blink sketch using File ⟩ Examples ⟩ Basics. Open it up and take a look. The first part is setup(), which does just what you'd expect—it gets the program elements ready to go. setup() runs once when the Arduino is powered up; as long as the power isn't shut off and restored, setup() won't rerun.

Here is the setup for Blink:

```
void setup() {
  pinMode(LED_BUILTIN, OUTPUT);
}
```

As you can see, setup() encompasses the area within the curly braces, which consists of one command: initializing the built-in LED's pin as an output pin.

Next let's consider loop(). Contrasting with the setup() function, loop() runs repeatedly until halted in software or the board loses power. It contains four commands: First, turn on the LED. Next, delay the sketch for a thousand microseconds—that is, 1 second. The third command tells the Arduino to turn off the LED, and the fourth delays the `loop()` function for another second:

```
void loop() {
  digitalWrite(LED_BUILTIN, HIGH);
  delay(1000);
  digitalWrite(LED_BUILTIN, LOW);
  delay(1000);
}
```

That's the sketch! Obviously they won't all be this simple.

Upload Sketches

Once you have a sketch open on your screen, follow these steps:

1. Select Arduino/Genuino UNO from the Tools > Boards dropdown menu.
2. Select a serial port from Tools > Port. Choose any one that works!
3. Before you upload, you might want to check the code by choosing Sketch > Verify/Compile, which will sniff out any errors without trying to upload.
4. Double-check that the USB cable is connected.
5. Click Sketch > Upload to send the sketch to the Arduino.

NEXT STEPS

Where to next? The best way to learn about Arduino and their projects is to explore the example sketches found with the Arduino software. Choosing File > Examples in the Arduino software takes you to a huge number of sketches illustrating how to do pretty much anything that can be done with the boards. Additionally, the Arduino Playground (playground.ardino.cc) offers help and suggestions for new and experienced programmers.

Index

CPSIA information can be obtained
at www.ICGtesting.com
Printed in the USA
BVOW07s1953040817

491097BV00002B/2/P